CHEERFUL CHRISTIANITY

A CHILD'S JOURNEY TO
FINDING JESUS

CHEERFUL CHRISTIANITY

A CHILD'S JOURNEY TO FINDING JESUS

OLIVIA RUTH BARNEY

CFI
An imprint of Cedar Fort, Inc.
Springville, Utah

ISBN 13: 978-1-4621-4243-9

Published by CFI, an imprint of Cedar Fort, Inc.
2373 W. 700 S., Springville, UT 84663
Distributed by Cedar Fort, Inc., www.cedarfort.com

Library of Congress Control Number: 2022933521

Cover design by Shawnda T. Craig

Printed in the United States of America

10 9 8 7 6 5 4 3 2 1

Printed on acid-free paper

To Missy, who left to do God's work in heaven,
and who was one of my greatest cheerleaders.

CONTENTS

"It is one thing to know that Jesus Christ came to earth to die for us. That is fundamental and foundational to the doctrine of Christ. But we also need to appreciate that the Lord desires, through His Atonement and by the power of the Holy Ghost, to live in us—not only to direct us but also to empower us."

—David A. Bednar

GLASS IN THE KITCHEN

She watched as the digital clock on the microwave changed from 4:47 to 4:48 a.m. The change in those small green numbers was brief and disappointing. Nothing was different. Nothing was ever different. She sat in the same quiet house, at the same kitchen table, offering the same unheard prayers to the same unresponsive God.

The Bible in front of her was open, but she wasn't reading it anymore. She was tired of reading about a Savior she didn't know; tired of hearing about miracles that didn't happen anymore. The sky outside was dark and overcast, and it hid both the stars and moon from view. It was too early in the day to be awake, yet too late in the night to go back to sleep. So, she sat there, staring at the glass of water in front of her, wondering why she could never quite fit in even with something as basic as maintaining a normal sleep schedule.

The condensation running down the side of the glass made her throat ache, and she swallowed hard, changing her focus back to the matter at hand with just a bit of effort. It was only a glass of water. Eight ounces of fluid that would make her healthier, stronger, and more capable of recovering. She was home. She was safe. There was absolutely no reason to be afraid.

Her stomach protested loudly, breaking the stillness around her and briefly waking the German shepherd who lay ever vigilant at her feet. Another growl from her stomach filled the air before it was silent once again. She hadn't eaten in almost seventy-two hours, but that wasn't abnormal anymore. The hollow feeling in her stomach, while unpleasant, had become familiar because it was still a preferable alternative to the other things she could be feeling.

She inhaled sharply and quickly put the glass of water to her lips before she could change her mind. Cool relief coated her tongue and soothed her dry throat. She swallowed back an involuntary whimper as she finished the last of her drink. An immediate longing for more settled inside her chest.

She didn't have an eating disorder, despite the things her classmates often whispered in the halls. She wasn't punishing herself for a standard of beauty that she couldn't attain. And she wasn't seeking attention the way her middle school teachers seemed to believe. On the contrary, nothing had made her feel more invisible or less understood.

But she didn't feel angry at them for the accusations they threw at her, primarily because it wasn't logical to be angry. She knew they didn't understand. They *couldn't* understand. Nobody expected a thirteen-year-old girl to sit alone and awake in the middle of the night, praying to a God for answers that didn't exist and for a body that didn't fail quite so often.

She avoided eating because food, all food, shut her body down. There was no pattern to the chaos, no consistency in her triggers. Her stomach was a ticking time bomb that sent shock waves of pain throughout every nerve in her body. Yes, the initial attack began within her gut, but it never stopped there. Instead, it spread, fast as wildfire in a season of drought, until even her fingertips shook from the effects.

She glanced at the clock again, its green numbers showing that ten minutes had passed. Warm hope filled her chest, and she moved to refill her glass with more of the divine liquid. She had never expected that the water from her tap would come to taste so ambrosial.

But the change occurred almost instantly.

One second, she was at the sink, allowing a small smile of relief to lift her cheeks, and the next she was on the ground, her body curled tightly into the fetal position, shards of glass littering the surrounding tile. A small puddle of water caused them to shine iridescently.

The beginnings of a scream rose in her throat, and she quickly covered her mouth to muffle the sound. Her dog was fully awake and alert now, hovering amid the glass and confusion with worry apparent in her movements. The water she'd swallowed only minutes before threatened to come back up, and she fought desperately to avoid vomiting. She had to keep something down. She was *determined* to keep it down.

Tears stained her cheeks and salted her lips, adding savor and substance to her appeal. She was praying to God again, begging for grace the same way she had each day for the last two years. He was ignoring her again, staying silent like He always did.

Sometimes she hated Him.

When she finally opened her eyes, they felt dry, and she wondered when the tears had stopped flowing. Her dog was watching her cautiously now, whimpering quietly in concerned question. The clock read 6:15 a.m. She should be getting ready for school.

A distant bedroom door opened, and she forced herself into motion before the rest of her family found her catatonic on the kitchen floor. She picked up the broken pieces of glass and used a small towel to absorb the remaining water. Moving to the bathroom, she splashed cool water on her face, removing all traces of tears from her cheeks.

She gazed at her reflection in the mirror and saw the defeated girl that stared back at her. Dark circles of exhaustion settled beneath panicked eyes, and her lips were cracked from dehydration. She had never loathed a child's face before, but she despised her own. So, with a steadying breath, she forced herself to smile until her eyes looked a little less hollow and cold.

The rules had changed again, as they so often did, and apparently water was no longer safe.

She longed to feel safe.

Instead, she felt fragile and broken; a damaged person living a damned life.

She shook her head to interrupt her thoughts. She didn't have time to feel angry at God; she would yell at Him later. For now, it was time to start over. Another day. Another facade.

She busied herself by getting ready for school, eventually leaving the house quietly and skipping breakfast once again. It wasn't hard to justify her actions. She did it automatically. Skipping breakfast was all right, necessary even, because she had a math test during first period. She couldn't afford to be sick until it was over.

All day, every day, she moved forward amid pain and fear. She didn't choose to. She had to. And this was her life.

This was *my* life.

For more than a decade, this is how I lived: alone, afraid, and accused of inventing the whole illness by pretty much everyone except my immediate family, primarily because I didn't always look the way you'd expect a constantly sick child to appear.

And it was hell.

Now that I'm away from it, I can look back with more objectivity and understanding. Of course, I still see the pain. I still see the girl who spent most of her conscious thoughts in personal prayer. But I also see a whole lot of grace and God that I couldn't always acknowledge in the heat of the moment. But He was there. I know that now.

For a long time, I testified of the grace of God privately, within my own church building and on my private social media accounts. I never wanted to share my story with the world because I didn't want the world to know me because of my illness. I wanted to separate myself from those experiences and simply forget. I would move on and never talk about it again.

But when you're twenty-three years old, a more than a decade of experiences becomes a hard thing to forget. The more I remember, the more I become convinced that my survival was only attained by the means of some divine intervention or godly grace.

Think about it. How did I survive going days between meals, drinking almost nothing, and barely resting without constantly being hospitalized? How did I get up every day for eleven years and live my own personal hell all over again? How did I endure the bullying and accusations from my peers and even my teachers? How did I physically, emotionally, and spiritually survive? It couldn't have been solely through my own resources. Most of the time my resources had long since been exhausted.

I can no longer testify of grace privately if I'm only doing so to avoid reliving a painful past. And I've experienced far too many miracles over the years to simply stay quiet altogether, especially when so many others are feeling just as lost and abandoned as I did at the time.

So, it's time to be brave for God.

It's time to be brave for you.

This is for all of us; a candid recollection of a child's journey to finding her Savior paired with key lessons I learned about heaven along the way.

This is my testimony. My story. My faith and fears laid out on the page.

So, if you find yourself awake in the middle of the night, questioning God and His grace, or desperately seeking that same Savior of old, I hope this helps. I never wrote this for me; it was always for you.

Prior to writing this book, I faced countless questions and doubts that were designed to hinder my progress and keep this book from seeing the light. What's even more frustrating is that none of those expressions of inadequacy came from the people around me. Instead, it was me. I was the one with the self-doubt. I was the only one who thought that writing a book about Jesus Christ was a task for someone far better than myself.

Many of you, after learning that I only turned twenty-three a few months ago, will probably wonder some of the same things that I wondered when I first felt the need to write this. You too will probably consider me inadequate. You too will probably wonder why I felt prompted to write this book at all. Or maybe you won't. But I wondered about those things.

I soon realized that if I allowed my own self-doubt to mix with fear and intimidation, it would keep me paralyzed from progression. But I did just that and often found myself at a loss on how to even begin.

One night was particularly bothersome. I hadn't attempted to work on this manuscript for several days, failing at my previous goal to designate two to three hours each day toward writing (an admittedly ambitious goal for a young college student). I was angry and frustrated with myself, and suddenly all of those previous insecurities flooded back into my stream of consciousness.

What makes me qualified to teach about something so great and central to all of our lives? What does someone as young as me have to offer? How can my voice and perspective possibly be significant? Surely there is someone better qualified and more educated for such a task.

I began to spiral into self-deprecation.

Fortunately, before I could continue down this train of thought any further, I felt the loving reprimand of the Spirit. Words of chastisement quickly entered my mind.

"What do eighteen-year-old men and nineteen-year-old women have to offer when they choose to serve missions? What makes their voices significant? Of course, there are people better suited for the task ahead, but I have a work for them to do. And as for your own qualifications on teaching such a topic, just what makes you think that you'll be doing the teaching?"

I was sufficiently humbled.

The next morning, I got to work with a newfound reminder that God will qualify His people to run His errands. So here I am, and here you are.

I'd like to add that this is primarily a narrative of how I understand and have come to understand Jesus Christ and His Atonement. I'm not claiming my words as doctrine. I've just had a unique set of challenges thus far in life that have motivated me to study Jesus and His role as my Savior. Your experiences won't be exactly like mine. My testimony has developed because of many personal moments with Him, and if I'm being honest, the idea of sharing those events with whoever picks up this book is slightly terrifying. But I feel compelled to do so anyway.

I was eleven years old when my parents and I really noticed that something was wrong, but I'd had a sensitive stomach long before then. At least, we assumed my stomach was merely sensitive. It didn't occur to anyone that there might actually be underlying health concerns until my symptoms grew more severe. I was in sixth grade, my final year of elementary school, when we started seeing doctors.

But let me back up briefly and introduce myself. I'm Olivia. I was born and raised in Utah as a member of The Church of Jesus Christ of Latter-day Saints, and yes, I'm a Christian. (That's a common misconception people have about our Church. We are indeed Christian, and we have so many more beliefs in common with you than you might think. But this is not a pitch for you to join my religion, so I'll leave it at that. We're just talking about Jesus here.)

Although I grew up in a religious household, I wasn't exempt from wondering if God even existed at all. As you'll soon find out, that was a question I wrestled with for years.

Our home was always busy and messy, but I didn't mind. There were nine of us there—my parents, five siblings, my aunt, and me. When you add in numerous dogs, cats, bunnies, and even frogs over the years, we were filled completely to the brim. Neighbor kids walked in and out of our house at all hours of the day and night as if it was their own home, and we liked it that way. They were our best friends, and I can recall many summer nights spent playing tag across an entire block of yards. We stayed out until the streetlights turned on and our parents called to us from the porch.

I normally came home covered in dirt and blood. I'm not sure how I did it, but nearly every day I managed to trip and scrape myself on the concrete. For the first seven years of my life, I can't recall many days where I *didn't* have cuts along my forehead and nose. (My neighbor's porch and I were enemies back then, though I'm still baffled that I managed to fall face first on their porch step three times a week.)

I've only become marginally more graceful since then.

I've always been kind of oblivious to my own limitations, which is important to know before we get into the details of this story. I've simply always believed that I was capable of doing the things I wanted to do. As a toddler (and okay, even now), this got me into trouble. I genuinely thought I could do *anything* and *everything* that my parents could. So, I dropped a lot of dishes, got lost in a million public places, and frequently took apart toys and electronics, just to see how they worked. I contributed greatly to my parents' exhaustion, but this confidence in my own abilities to overcome setbacks played a key role in my survival of what we now call "the sick years."

It's impossible for me to give you all the nitty-gritty details of my experiences over the last ten or eleven years, and I wouldn't want to. Most of the days were dark, painful, and pretty much an exact repeat of the story I began this book with. (True, I didn't break a glass *every* night. But most of my days consisted of starving in public just to weep in private. At night you could find me rocking in the fetal position or lying on the cold bathroom floor, waiting for another wave of pain to pass.) I wouldn't want you to read that. (And I certainly don't want to write it.) So, I'm picking the highlights. The most important and significant moments. The times that changed my spirituality.

This brings me to my final piece of introductory information: the title, *Cheerful Christianity.* Though I am an admittedly positive person, a decade of debilitating pain was anything *but* cheerful. And that's why I picked this title. There's a misconception among religious communities that faithful discipleship leads to constant joy and enlightenment. While being a disciple of Christ certainly does bring happiness and light into your life, the absence of those blessings does not mean you're a bad disciple. I am a cheerful Christian but not because life is easy, or because I feel the constant guidance of my Savior. Instead, I am cheerful because with Christ I'm enough. So maybe cheerful Christianity doesn't refer to being happy or positive all the time. Maybe cheerful Christianity refers to finally feeling whole.

CAN GOD LOVE A BROKEN PERSON?

I'm kind of a mess.

I don't think I've met a single individual who actually *liked* middle school gym class. It was a time of humiliation for most of us, and how could it not be? Gather a large group of young, self-conscious teenagers, make them change into the most unflattering clothes imaginable, and force them to show their peers how physically inept they really were.

Okay, maybe not everyone felt that way, but I did. I disliked everything about gym class, but to be completely honest, I didn't participate all that much. By the time I reached seventh grade, my symptoms were a little like this: I experienced near constant aching of my joints. I was hungry—so, so hungry—but everything I ate came right back up. Because gym class was right after lunch, I spent most days in the locker room, vomiting, praying my friends didn't walk in, and wishing I was anywhere else.

But it wasn't long before my peers began to notice, and I wanted to disappear from embarrassment.

It's hard to forgive your body at any age when it can't properly function. But as a child, with friends who teased me for having an eating disorder (which I didn't actually have), I couldn't do anything else but hate my body.

And I continued to hate it all through middle school as my symptoms got worse. Soon I was vomiting in trash cans in public places because that's all that was available. I walked out of most of my classes at least once a day to rush to the restroom or to take a few minutes to cry by myself in an empty hallway because my pain was so severe that I couldn't hold my pencil.

By the end of my ninth-grade year, a couple of my nineteen doctors (yes, you read that right) came up with some reasons I might be ill. First, my gallbladder didn't function, which made it harder to digest certain kinds of food. Second, I was diagnosed with Juvenile Rheumatoid Arthritis (JRA), which explained the joint pain.

So, I was taken in for surgery, had my gallbladder removed, and started medication for the JRA. And I felt better. I praised God for the first time in years because He had healed me . . . for about a month.

My symptoms returned, stronger than before, and we spent more long and painful years trying to find answers. By my first year of college, I'd tried pretty much every diet imaginable, and nothing worked. I spent many days inside the lab for tests, scans, blood draws, colonoscopies, endoscopies, ultrasounds, and more. But slowly, over the course of my first four years of college, we found real answers.

My body was riddled with infection. I'm not sure how we'd missed it, but it had been there for years. My tonsils in particular were badly infected, which meant I swallowed infection hundreds of times each day. I had stomach ulcers and parasites, both of which required extensive medicinal and dietetic treatments. I'd grown out of my JRA at this point but was diagnosed with fibromyalgia in its place.

I had a hiatal hernia, which essentially meant that my stomach had moved and was going through my diaphragm. It made it hard to breathe and caused instant pain when I ate.

And to top off my list of medical anomalies, I was also allergic to about 33 percent of the world. Things like iron, calcium, the B vitamins. I was allergic to dairy, grains, sugars, vitamin C, yeast, eggs, grass, and so much more. No wonder I couldn't find any type of food that was safe. My body never stood a chance.

So, I spent years undergoing treatments for allergies, parasites, and ulcers. I had surgery on my stomach to fix the hernia, had my tonsils removed, and had an additional surgery to remove excess infection that didn't lie in my tonsils. I got on medication to help manage my fibromyalgia, though it's likely something I'll have to live with.

And while I felt a million times better after all of this, I still wasn't better.

Now, don't get frustrated and close the book. I promise that eventually things did get better for me. But I have to stop my medical history here so we can talk about the one reason you're reading this—Jesus.

Because for over a decade, I prayed earnestly for answers that didn't come. And that was a difficult concept for me to understand. My little adolescent brain couldn't fathom why God would ignore my prayers and pleadings. Didn't He hear me? Didn't He love me? I had spent my whole childhood believing that He did, but suddenly I was second guessing the very foundational doctrines of my testimony.

Looking back, I can see how obviously God was manifesting His love for me. In the heat of the moment, however, I was blind to every single one of His love letters. (That never stopped God from sending them, though. I don't think He'll ever stop trying to love and bless us, even if we never love Him back. It's a pretty miraculous concept when you think about it).

But all of those unanswered prayers? That's when I began to hate Him.

How could God be loving and merciful? If He were truly my Father, then how could He look upon my failing body and broken heart and allow the breaking to continue? What parent, with the power to take every ounce of it away, would allow their child to endure something so horrible and painful, especially beginning at age eleven?

No parent would. No parent *could.*

So, it couldn't be true. God couldn't, and surely didn't, love me. He didn't care about how much pain I was in. He didn't really hear my prayers. And if He did, then He chose to ignore them.

For the first few months, I let myself get angrier and angrier. Though it probably sounds odd, I don't regret a second of that. I spoke forcefully with God in those months. Nobody tells you that's okay to do, but I think it is. For me, it was a very necessary interaction to have with Him.

I don't regret being angry at God. I don't regret the hours I spent yelling at Him because over time I watched that yelling turn to crying, crying turn to pleading, and pleading eventually turn to submission.

I don't regret being angry because I needed a chance to grieve. Grieve the injustice of it all. Grieve my childhood that was quite suddenly and forcefully replaced by the cold realities of living in an imperfect and unjust world.

Eventually I realized that God was all I had. If medical professionals couldn't help me, and I couldn't help myself, then God was my only other option. I remember that moment when things changed for me. I remember thinking, *Okay, God; you win. Let's try this your way.*

Hating God was probably one of the most confusing and emotionally draining experiences of my life, but I'm so grateful for it. I'm grateful that I was angry and that I put so much effort into hating God, because it was the quickest way for me to realize that I was wrong. He wasn't to blame for my pain. He didn't enjoy watching me suffer. And now I can quite confidently say that *every* time I cried, He cried too. Every. Single. Time.

I continued to pray for health, but I also started to put more energy into studying the gospel and in learning if what I'd been taught was true. Was I really a daughter of God?

Because if I *was* a daughter of God, then surely He loved me. And *if* He loved me, then surely He didn't enjoy watching me suffer. So there had to be some greater purpose in it all. But again, that was all entirely dependent on if I was truly *His.*

Although my team of doctors focused on managing my pain levels, I focused on something else: managing my faith. Developing a testimony of my own divinity soon became essential for me, and it changed the entire course of my life. As that testimony grew, I didn't feel quite so small and weak. Knowing who I was to God changed the way I saw myself, others, and even my circumstances. It became the rock that I could hold on to when everything else came crashing down and I wanted nothing more than a sliver of peace. For the first time in my life, I had access to more power than I had ever had before. And that extra power is what we commonly refer to as grace.

SEEKING A SAVIOR

GETTING TO KNOW JESUS

I've always believed in Jesus. I grew up singing about Him, learning the stories of His miracles, and praying for a miracle of my own because I assumed He could give it to me. But I only knew *about* Him; I didn't actually know who He was, let alone who He could be to me.

I soon realized that if you want to know and understand Jesus Christ, you actually have to spend time with Him.

And if you want to be like Jesus Christ, you have to spend time doing the things that He would do.

So, I studied Him. I read His words and the words of the prophets and apostles who testified of Him. I asked questions about Him, prayed to God to feel close to Him, and tried my best to build a relationship with Him.

I began by reading scripture stories from the New Testament. Have you ever noticed that it's much easier to understand the character of a person if you can see how they treat other people? This is especially telling when they aren't trying to impress anyone. (Think about the people who serve strangers when they think that no one is looking. That tells you a lot about their true nature and their honest intentions.)

Fortunately, the New Testament is all about Christ's interactions with the people around Him. And even more fortunate for us, we have multiple accounts of these events, which means that we have multiple perspectives on who Christ really was on Earth and who He can be to us today.

Maybe it's just because I was sick and in need of healing myself, but one of the first things I noticed is that Christ truly *was* a healer. He healed bodies. He healed hearts. We have so many records of these miracles, so I'd be willing to guess that most of us are comfortable with that idea. We'd be content calling Him a healer. And we're comfortable calling Him that because we're familiar with the many stories of Him healing the sick, restoring vision to the blind, and even raising the dead. And because we're so familiar with this side of Jesus Christ, I won't spend too much time on it. Instead, I'll simply recommend that you take the time to read, or perhaps reread, those accounts. My three personal favorites are listed in the next chapter because I resonate the most with them, but there are certainly others you could include in your study. Regardless, here's a starting point.

ACCOUNTS OF CHRIST HEALING

CHRIST HEALS THE MAN SICK WITH PALSY

(Matthew 9:1–8; Mark 2:1–12; Luke 5:18–26)

Picture a man physically paralyzed, emotionally exhausted, and undoubtedly spiritually spent. He's accustomed to living like this, but that doesn't mean he has stopped praying for things to be different. He hears stories, rumors really, of a great man who has the power to heal all manner of illnesses. This man claims to be the Son of God. He says He is here to save His people.

If true, this would be remarkable, something to celebrate. And if true, then maybe this sick man could be made whole. But he cannot go to see the Son of God for himself. He's paralyzed, after all.

Four loved ones carry him to meet their Savior. They encounter crowds of people and are unable to push through the masses. But they can't give up now. Christ is their friend's only hope, and they couldn't possibly turn away when help was almost within their reach.

So instead of fighting the crowds, they lower this sick man down from the roof above, and when Christ sees the lengths they went to just to reach Him, He praises their faith and heals the paralytic.

This story is the one I think of first when someone says that Christ can heal both body and soul. In fact, when Christ sees the man sick with palsy, it is his *spiritual* health that our Savior addresses first, saying, "Son, thy sins be forgiven thee" (Mark 2:5).

It isn't until after the scribes question His authority to forgive sin that Christ heals the man's physical ailments. To those scribes Christ says, "Why reason ye these things in your hearts? Whether it is easier to say to the sick of the palsy, Thy sins be forgiven thee; or to say, Arise, and take up thy bed, and walk? But that ye may know that the Son of man hath power on earth to forgive sins, (he saith to the sick of the palsy,) I say unto thee, Arise, and take up thy bed, and go thy way into thine house" (Mark 2:8–11).

The scriptures tell us that the man immediately arose and did exactly that.

Can you imagine the joy that he felt that day to be healed, not only physically but spiritually as well? Can you imagine the excitement that it brought his friends and family to see him whole, especially after having been burdened for so long? And more important than any of those other things, we should consider the why behind those questions.

Why would it bring them joy and excitement? *Why* were all the people amazed at this miracle? It's because Christ gave this man what no one else could give him. No doctor or priest could offer the same type of healing that he had just received. Only Jesus Christ could offer that to him. Miracles can only be given through Christ, or through the power of Christ, because He is our connection to heaven. And a miracle occurs when we are given something that only heaven could give, be that healing, strength, and so on.

CHRIST RAISES JAIRUS'S DAUGHTER FROM THE DEAD

(Matthew 9:18–19, 23–26; Mark 5:21–24, 35–43; Luke 8:41–42, 49–56)

This story is told in two parts. In the first part, Jairus, a local ruler, begs Jesus to heal his young daughter who was so ill that everyone feared she would die. This was a time-sensitive matter, and Jairus, surely motivated by the anxiety of a helpless father, implores Christ to run and rescue his child. In the second part, Christ brings her back to life, having arrived at their house too late and after she had already passed away.

Do you think Jairus was heartbroken at the news of his daughter's passing? Undoubtedly. Was he angry with Jesus? Most likely. Did he blame Jesus (at least in part) for the death of his daughter? If I had to guess, I'd say yes.

I like this account *because* it's broken up. Christ healed another on His way to save Jairus's daughter. To Jairus, it seemed that Christ had failed. He was too late. He didn't listen, or maybe He didn't care enough. He didn't run to his aid, but instead took His time by stopping to talk to (and heal) another. And now Jairus's daughter was gone, unreachable and unsavable from the chains of death.

But it wasn't too late. When it comes to godly matters, it is *never* too late. Christ brought her back. He answered Jairus's initial pleading. And I'm sure it wasn't in the way that Jairus wanted. In fact, he had specifically asked Christ to *save* his daughter from death. Christ agreed to do so. And while I'm sure Jairus had meant that he wanted his daughter to be healed *before* she died, the fact of the matter remains that the Lord *did* fulfill His promise. He *did* save her from death. Part of the reason I love this story so much is that it teaches us that yes, the Lord hears and answers our prayers, but we must also be willing to have faith in His ways and His timing.

CHRIST HEALS THE WOMAN WITH THE ISSUE OF BLOOD

(Matthew 9:20–22; Mark 5:25–34; Luke 8:43–48)

This is the story that drove my incessant hope and desire to be healed. This story hit home to me because this woman had been ill for twelve years. She had "spent all that she had" and "suffered many things of physicians" to no avail (Mark 5:26).

I could relate to that. Sure, I was only sick for eleven years, but in the midst of pain, it felt like an eternity. I too spent all that I had. My parents and I spent all that we had financially. I certainly spent all that I had physically. And I quite often spent all that I had spiritually and emotionally. I had also "suffered many things of physicians" (Mark 5:26). I had endured countless surgeries and procedures, tests and scans. Some of were easy, requiring just a few minutes of time or a few vials of blood. But some of the things they had to do took hours out of my day or were so painful and difficult that I still start shaking as I think back on them all these years later.

So, I understood her. I understood how to live with pain. I understood how desperately she wanted to be healed. And I understood how terrifying it must have been for her to think that maybe she would be stuck like this forever. Maybe healing would never come. Maybe she was just going to have to be brave for now and hope for things to be made right in the eternities. Having to face that possible reality is both terrifying and heartbreaking. I've been there.

Imagine the almost painful, sudden rush of hope that must have filled her chest when she realized that her Savior was nearby. And not just near but quite literally within her reach. Should she reach for Him? Did she even dare to try?

I love her example of faith because she didn't need to speak to Christ or have His hands rest upon her head. She didn't need signs and angels to convince her of His majesty. She just believed. And because she believed, she knew that all she needed to do was reach for Him. She just needed to touch Him. She understood Christ's power so extensively that she knew that merely touching the hem of His robe held enough power to heal her.

As if that wasn't inspiring enough, the way that Christ responds to her small act of faith leaves me almost breathless. Although He was surrounded by people, He noticed her. He was aware of her faith. He was aware of her outstretched hand. And the very moment she reached for His robe, He responded with love, compassion, and encouragement.

He was on His way to heal someone else—Jairus's daughter, in fact. He was in a hurry to save another life. Surely, He didn't need to stop and speak with her, especially when touching His robe would have been enough to make her whole. Surely what happened next wasn't necessary. And maybe it wasn't necessary, but it was still important.

Because despite His rush, He took the time to talk with her. Despite the fact that He had other work to do, He set aside time for her and her alone. He healed her. He praised her faith. He encouraged her to continue on in righteousness. And I don't know about you, but I think that says a *lot* about Him.

AS LONG AS IT IS THE NATURE OF MAN TO FAIL, IT WILL BE THE NATURE OF CHRIST TO FORGIVE

We can learn a lot about the character and nature of Jesus Christ simply by looking at those three stories from the New Testament. In the first story, we learned that Christ can heal both body and soul, and that a miracle occurs when Christ gives us something, or power to do something, that we could not otherwise obtain without Him.

In the second story, we learn that Christ fulfills His promises in His own time and in His own way. Blessings and answers may not always come quickly, but as we rely on Jesus Christ, they *will* come. He has not forgotten you just because He stops to help another on His way.

And in the third story, we learn that Christ values us individually. He takes, and has taken, time for each of us. He wants to talk to us. He wants to heal us. He wants to encourage us to continue to become better. He is not too busy to listen to you. He is not too burdened to help carry your load.

Those three stories alone show us the true nature of Jesus Christ, but the scriptures are full of many more accounts that illustrate who He really is. I encourage you to take the time to study those stories, to pray to know of their truth, and to start developing a personal relationship with your Savior. Dive into the scriptures and let them become alive in you, because they aren't just nice stories. They're life histories and promises for the future. Start today, because knowing Him is essential for understanding His love and grace.

As you get to know Jesus Christ personally, it becomes a little bit easier to understand His atoning act. Everything Christ has ever been recorded doing was done in love. Every blessing He gave was given through love. Every doctrine He taught with a love for God's children and a sincere desire to bring them home. Even His rebuking and reprimanding words were spoken because Christ loves us too much to watch us destroy our chances of eternal happiness. Christ emulates love. Christ *is* love. And when you start to see Him as an embodiment of the purest form of godly love, the idea that He would atone for the people He loves starts to seem a little less incredulous.

Of course, even if you believe Christ loves His people enough to save them, it doesn't have much effect on you until you believe that you're worth saving.

I know, that's easier said than done.

One of the reasons grace is such a hard concept for most people to comprehend is that most of us don't feel like we're worthy of being saved. We aren't worth the trouble. We've messed up too many times. We're too far gone. If people knew the things we've said, done, or thought, they would agree. We don't deserve much of anything.

But those are all lies; clever lies that we believe literally all the time.

Your Heavenly Father and Savior *do* know everything you've said, done, or thought. You aren't hiding anything from them. They are fully aware of how imperfect you are. They already know that you've messed up a million times and that you'll probably mess up a billion more. They know all of that and they love you anyway. They see you as valuable anyway. They want to save you *anyway*. Jeffrey R. Holland expounds upon the love that God has for you and me in a very poignant way. He says,

"My brothers and sisters, the first great commandment of all eternity is to love God with all of our heart, might, mind, and strength—that's the first great commandment. But the first great truth of all eternity is that God loves us with all of His heart, might, mind, and strength. That love is the foundation stone of eternity, and it should be the foundation stone of our daily life. Indeed it is only with that reassurance burning in our soul that we can have the confidence to keep trying to improve, keep seeking forgiveness for our sins, and keep extending that grace to our neighbor."[1]

One thing I've learned is that the gospel of Jesus Christ never has been, and never will be, about what we deserve. If we continue to keep score and weigh our good deeds against our bad ones, we'll come up short every time. It will never look good for us on paper because we fail so consistently. But it isn't about that. It never has been.

Christ is the purest source of love. We saw that as we looked at some of the stories of Him in the New Testament. He is love, and it is love that is at the center of this gospel. It is love that is at the center of God's plan. So, throw out your unreasonable expectations for yourself and forget about what you and I deserve. We'll never deserve the blessings that the Lord offers us, but He'll offer them anyway because He thinks you're worth loving. But do you? Remember, the Lord doesn't need us. He wants us.

I learned a lot about the Atonement of Jesus Christ from my New Testament professor at Brigham Young University. I'll never forget the fierceness in my professor's eyes as he bore his testimony of Jesus Christ and His role as our Savior.

I distinctly remember several students raising their hands and asking a series of what-if type questions. These were mostly questions about what Christ's Atonement would *not* cover. They wanted to know how the Atonement could possibly apply to those of us who are already too far gone.

My faithful professor interrupted their line of questioning abruptly, though not unkindly. He just very firmly replied, "Christ's Atonement encompasses all. What Christ creates, He saves."

He repeated this testament with every what-if question that was asked.

---

1. Jeffrey R. Holland, "Tomorrow the Lord Will do Wonders Among You," April 2016 general conference, https://www.churchofjesuschrist.org/study/general-conference/2016/04/tomorrow-the-lord-will-do-wonders-among-you?lang=eng

I realized that there aren't any exceptions to what Christ can heal. If there were, His Atonement would not be considered perfect or infinite. He covered everything. He paid the price for all things, past, present, and future. The only way He cannot save you is if you refuse to accept His grace. So, if you're ever doubting whether you can be forgiven for a mistake you've made, or redeemed after continually falling short, ask yourself the following question: Did He create me? Because if He did, then He'll save you too.

OUR SOURCE OF STRENGTH

I spent a long time studying grace because it was hard for me to comprehend. Where does grace come from? Why does it have power? The Bible Dictionary tells us that it is given through the "bounteous mercy and love of Jesus Christ." But what does that really mean? Does Jesus Christ really love us enough to forgive us of our sins?

Most definitions of love have to do with a concern for another person's well-being. This concern for another person is generally deemed as unselfish, loyal, or benevolent. And I agree with most of that. I think pure love (and surely godly love) should be unselfish, unconditional, and unending. What this kind of definition does not mention, however, is the power that this type of love gives us. It enables us to do more, be more, and become more. And I'm not even talking about religious commitment yet. I'm talking about the kind of love that most of us have felt for another person at some point in time.

In April of 2014, W. Craig Zwick gave an address entitled "What Are You Thinking?" in which he gave a fantastic, real-life example of what pure love looks like. As this was his own firsthand experience, I'll skip the synopsis and let you read straight from the source. He tells the story much more effectively than I ever could.

"Forty-one years ago I climbed into the driver's seat of an 18-wheel semi-truck with my beautiful wife, Jan, and our infant son, Scotty. We were taking a heavy load of construction materials across several states.

"In those days there were no seat-belt restrictions or infant car seats. My wife held our precious son in her arms. Her comment "We sure are high off the ground" should have given me a clue about her feelings of apprehension.

"As we made our descent over historic Donner Pass, a steep section of highway, the cab of the semi suddenly and unexpectedly filled with thick smoke. It was difficult to see, and we could hardly breathe.

"With a heavy rig, brakes alone are not enough to rapidly decrease speed. Using the engine brakes and gearing down, I frantically attempted to stop.

"Just as I was pulling to the side of the road, but before we had come to a full stop, my wife opened the door of the cab and jumped out with our baby in her arms. I watched helplessly as they tumbled in the dirt.

"As soon as I had the semi stopped, I bolted from the smoking cab. With adrenaline pumping, I ran through the rocks and weeds and held them in my arms. Jan's forearms and elbows were battered and bleeding, but thankfully she and our son were both breathing. I just held them close as the dust settled there on the side of the highway.

"As my heartbeat normalized and I caught my breath, I blurted out, "What in the world were you thinking? Do you know how dangerous that was? You could have been killed!"

"She looked back at me, with tears running down her smoke-smudged cheeks, and said something that pierced my heart and still rings in my ears: "I was just trying to save our son."

"I realized in that moment she thought the engine was on fire, fearing the truck would explode and we would die. I, however, knew it was an electrical failure—hazardous but not fatal. I looked at my precious wife, softly rubbing the head of our infant son, and wondered what kind of woman would do something so courageous."

What kind of woman would do something so courageous? The kind of woman who felt an immeasurable amount of love for her child. In that moment, that love became more than just a warm feeling. It became an actual source of power that gave her the strength and courage to go against her basic survival instincts and do something that would put her own life at risk just for the chance to save someone she loved.

It's this love that drives fathers and mothers to leave their families in defense of their country. It's this love that strengthens a young adult as they work two or three jobs to support their younger siblings. It's this love that motivates us to do things for others that we maybe wouldn't even do for ourselves.

Grace, this extra strength and help, is powered by love.

In 2018, Russell M. Nelson talked about four gifts that Jesus Christ offers to us, the first being love. He said, "First, He gave you and me an unlimited capacity to love. That includes the capacity to love the unlovable and those who not only do not love you but presently persecute and despitefully use you."[2]

I think about how difficult it is to love my siblings when they're being unkind, my neighbor when they've done something offensive, or those random strangers who seem to want me to fail. I think about how much better I could be at loving them. I think about how much better I could be at loving myself too.

But if you and I, as very imperfect human beings, have an unlimited capacity to love, then how much more can Jesus Christ, as the only perfect one among us, love?

His love is infinite. His love is unrestrained. His love is without bounds or limitations. It isn't something we have to earn. It is simply always there, independent of our actions. He loves us because we are His.

If love is a source of power that allows us to do more, give more, and be more, and if Christ is an unlimited source of that love and power, then grace makes a little bit more sense. It's essentially a source of heavenly help that's made possible and available to us by the unlimited love that Jesus Christ has for us. Grace isn't something that we're

---

2. Russell M. Nelson, "Four Gifts That Jesus Christ Offers to You," First Presidency Christmas Devotional, Dec. 2018, https://www.churchofjesuschrist.org/media/video/2018-12-0040-president-russell-m-nelson?lang=eng

going to run out of. We aren't going to use up all of our chances. We aren't going to hit a maximum number of times that we're allowed to ask for help or receive forgiveness. We have endless opportunities to partake of the grace of Jesus Christ because grace is infinite. The love that makes grace possible is infinite. Christ will never run out of love because love is the one of the few things that you can *always* create more of when you need it.

WHAT DOES GRACE FEEL LIKE TO YOU?

Grace feels different for each one of us. That makes sense when you consider that each of us feel and give love in different ways. It feels different for me depending on my circumstances and what type of help I need. When I'm in pain, grace feels like a warm embrace, and it gives me comfort that things will be all right. When I'm too exhausted to do the things I need to do, grace feels like a little extra strength, a little extra encouragement, and a little extra push in the right direction. I feel grace in little doses almost constantly, but maybe it doesn't feel like that to you.

For my ancestors, grace was the hope and reassurance that their family would make it to Zion safely. It was recognized in the moments when they felt like someone was helping push their handcarts, though they couldn't see anyone there.

Prior to writing this book, I asked my friends, family, and neighbors in an anonymous survey what grace felt like to them. It was a difficult question to answer, and many people told me that they didn't know. They weren't sure they had ever felt it before. But many others testified that they *did* know what grace felt like to them. They were confident that they *had* felt it at work in their lives. With their permission, I'll list some of their responses.

GRACE FEELS LIKE:

- "A weight being removed from my shoulders and receiving a peaceful reassurance of God's love and plan for me."
- "Grace feels like hope. Hope that I can do better and that who I am will be enough in the end."

- "Grace is the feeling of God's love, even when you know you've messed up. It's like a parent saying, 'It's okay. You'll get it right next time.'"
- "Peace seeped in strength. When grace fills me, I feel confident and strong."
- "It feels like love."
- "It's an enabling power that allows me to do everything that I can do, but it's also the power that covers everything I cannot or do not do. It is the power Christ used to save me."

If you aren't sure what grace feels like to you, that's okay. It took me a long time to identify what grace is and how it feels to me. The whole purpose of this book is to give you a starting point to discover that grace for yourself. In the end, what I write may or may not even make a difference. Your experiences will be different from mine. Your story is different from mine. And your relationship with Jesus Christ is different from mine.

My entire goal is to help you realize that your relationship with Jesus Christ is worth investing in. It's worth it to get to know Him. In fact, I can't think of anything else more important. Get to know Him. Study His character and figure out what kind of person He is. What is your relationship with Him? Personally, I feel like He's my best friend. But it took years of getting to know Him, dedicating time to Him, and trying to trust Him before I could confidently say that He *is* my best friend.

Your relationship with Jesus Christ will take time. It will take work. It will take sacrifices and probably some heartache on your part. But it also took sacrifices and heartache on His part. He sacrificed everything to get to know you, to save you, and to bring you home. So, sacrifice a few minutes each day. Give up that show or that habit that doesn't align with His teachings. Dedicate time to Him and His gospel. I promise that as you consistently work on developing a relationship with Him, your life will get better. You will be happier. You will become closer to who you want to be.

It'll be hard. Your trials won't immediately go away. You'll probably feel a significant amount of pushback from the adversary. I'm feeling that pushback even as I'm writing this. But trust me when I tell you that it will be the best investment of your life.

UNDERSTANDING CHRIST'S ATONEMENT

A PERSONAL ACT

One of the most wonderful people I've ever known taught me about Christ's Atonement. Or rather, he taught me to believe in it and make it personal to me. His name was Tony. He was one of the youth leaders in my church when I was growing up.

I admired Tony pretty much my whole life for a couple of reasons. First, Tony lived and breathed the teachings of Jesus Christ. He just understood the gospel in a way that I've never seen before. A quiet, but powerful, confidence emanated from him, and it came from his trust in the Lord. It was unlike anything I've ever seen, and I hope that one day I can have as much faith and trust in God as he did. But the second reason I admired Tony was that he understood people.

Tony could see a broken heart, a struggling soul, or someone who just felt invisible, and he would come to their rescue without delay. It was incredible. It didn't matter how good you were at hiding your fears or pain, Tony could see you. He could see your heart. And he didn't hesitate to reach out to you.

I've often wondered how he did that. How could he just *know* what you were feeling? How could he look at a person and immediately connect with them? How could he possibly know what words to say in that moment or how an individual needed to be loved?

I'm still in awe of his ability to do that. As I spent more time with him and learned from him, however, I realized that the spiritual veil we all passed through when entering mortality seemed thinner around him somehow. When Tony was around, a very tangible spirit of peace and happiness came with him. It was as if you could *feel* his testimony. Even if he wasn't verbally testifying to you, his life was a testament in and of itself. His heart, his spirit, and his life had been changed by the Atonement of Jesus Christ, and it was noticeable.

Because of this, learning from him was an absolute delight.

When I was a senior in high school, I struggled with my testimony more than I cared to admit. This was well after I had decided to trust God and wasn't angry at Him anymore. I just felt hopeless. In those months I was having a very hard time holding on to my belief that things would get better. My hope for a brighter future had diminished almost entirely.

It was a dark time for me. I was lonelier than I had been in quite a long time. My body continued to wage a civil war every time I ate, and each potential treatment just made the pain increase.

It was during these darker months that my friends and I received word that our Sunday School teachers would be moving away. We didn't know who our new teacher would be, but I found myself hoping it would be Tony. I prayed earnestly for him to fill that role, and much to my surprise and satisfaction, Tony was indeed called to be our new Sunday School teacher.

He created a safe environment. He welcomed our questions about the gospel and encouraged us to express our doubts. He wanted us to seek answers in a healthy way, and he wanted to help us search for those answers too. He didn't want us to have to do it alone. As I learned from him, I felt my shaking testimony begin to stand steady once again.

I can very clearly recall one Sunday School lesson he taught because it was the lesson that single-handedly changed my experience with the Atonement of Jesus Christ. As we talked about that pivotal event, Tony made it clear to us that Christ has atoned for me, for you, and for each of us. He made it evident that Christ's atoning sacrifice was done for us personally because we matter to Him individually.

This was a breakthrough concept for me, and I remember talking to Tony more in depth after our lesson. It wasn't that I was surprised that Christ atoned for me. It's just that I had never felt like the Atonement was particularly *personal.* After talking with Tony, however, my perspective completely changed.

It's my personal belief that Christ didn't atone for us all at once in one seemingly eternal moment. I think He atoned for each of us individually. He died for me. And then He died for you. And then He died for the next person, metaphorically. In doing this, each of us got the chance to put our arms around Him as He trembled in the garden. We got the opportunity to thank Him, kiss Him, and strengthen Him.

Maybe that it isn't how it happened at all, but it does make a lot of sense to me. The Atonement can sometimes seem incomprehensible. The idea of Christ experiencing everything, for every person, all at once seems impossible. And more than that, it's impersonal. It doesn't seem as significant to me if everything Christ felt for me was somehow jumbled in the mix of everyone else's sorrows. How can He truly know my pain or my sins if they were never distinguished from anyone else's?

But imagine that there was a part of His Atonement where He atoned for no one else except you. That was your moment. And in that moment, He felt and experienced every emotion you've ever felt, every temptation, every consequence that resulted from your actions. And in that moment, when Christ suffered solely for you, when He trembled and bled and cried out for His Father, you were there. You got a chance to be the angel supporting Him, holding Him, and strengthening Him with your profound gratitude alone.

Now doesn't that seem more personal? Can't you imagine that? I can. It makes sense to me. Again, I don't know what really happened in that garden. This is what makes the most sense to me, but in the end, it doesn't really matter how you picture it. Just picture it. What's most important is that you think about it, utilize it, and feel so grateful for it that you strive to keep Christ with you constantly.

Lessons with Tony helped me to personalize the Atonement of Jesus Christ and led to me developing a deeper, more meaningful relationship with my Savior. I can't tell you with certainty how those events really occurred. I wasn't there. And if I was, well, I can't remember. But regardless of how Christ's Atonement really went, I think it's important to explore various views of that sacrifice. Doing so will not only help you to appreciate the gift of grace more abundantly, but it will also help you to appreciate Jesus Christ more fully.

Tony taught me that.

This gospel is personal. Yes, we're sent here in families. Yes, we surround ourselves with friends and church members to help us do what is right and get back home. But in the end, the gospel of Jesus Christ is a personal thing. It's about you and your relationship with heaven. Your spirituality is your own. It is your responsibility. Your relationship with God is entirely up to you.

In 2018, I had one of my more significant surgeries on my stomach. We were hoping for this to be my miracle surgery. We were hoping that it would be the final puzzle piece that would lead to my healing. I was told that the first eight weeks would be extremely difficult, but because of a complication that took place about a week after surgery, in which my stomach became temporarily paralyzed, my eight-week recovery turned into twelve.

Even the simplest tasks took all of my energy, and for the most part, I was bound to my apartment. I had just moved in a few days before this surgery took place, so I didn't know many people yet. It was lonely and maddening to spend most of my time at home by myself. I hated it.

On Sundays, I tried my best to attend my church meetings, but most of the time I could only make it through an hour before my pain got out of hand and I needed to leave. But twelve weeks with minimal church attendance left my spirit pretty unhappy, until I realized that it was my responsibility, and no one else's, to find spiritual nourishment, regardless of if I could attend all of my Sunday meetings.

So, I started small by studying a less familiar chapter of scripture while I was stuck at home. When my roommates would come home from church, they would tell me what they learned, and slowly gospel discussions became a more prominent part of our home-life.

I will be forever grateful for my friends, family, and roommates for teaching me how to incorporate the gospel in my everyday life, because now we study and discuss the gospel together almost daily. Russell M. Nelson warned us that the adversary is increasing his attacks against us at an exponential rate, and I can feel that. I feel the adversary pushing back so hard. But as I work on improving my daily application of the gospel, I can also feel my Father in Heaven blessing me more than ever before, and certainly more than I deserve.

So, as we dive into our study of the Atonement of Jesus Christ, I'd like to add my voice of encouragement. You *can* have a personal relationship with Jesus Christ and with your Heavenly Parents. You *can* improve and become everything Heaven wants you to be. You *can* develop a testimony of your own. You *will* be blessed as you strive to do so.

Make it personal. Make your relationship with Jesus Christ your top priority. Put effort into that. As you do, blessings will come. Faith will come. A testimony will come. (Or maybe, in some cases, come back.)

THE ATONING ACT

The life and death of Jesus Christ changed history. His actions while on Earth, and His teachings after being resurrected, are crucial for succeeding in our own journey home. His Atonement single-handedly changed the outcome for every one of our stories. That sacrifice brought the very concept of hope into the world. It was born when He was.

It's important to recognize, however, that the Atonement, while significant, is significant *because* of Jesus Christ. That event changed history because Christ did. He performed the act. His grace was the power behind it.

For this reason, I've been working on only referring to that sacrifice as "the Atonement of Jesus Christ," not "the Atonement." I'm trying to remember His name in it. I'm trying to give it back to Him because it is, after all, entirely made possible through Him.

So, as we move forward, I'm going to try not to shorten the name of Christ's atoning act or remove His name from it. I think that it's something to at least think about.

As I first thought about this book and what I could possibly write that would be of value to someone else, I thought back upon my own experiences with Christ and His Atonement. What had He done for me? How does this act allow me to change? How am I personally affected by this?

The resulting list of answers overwhelmed me. I was stunned to see how fully and completely Christ and His Atonement have affected my life for the better. And as I sorted through my jumbled thoughts and experiences, I realized that much of what I want to talk about can be broken down into four categories: redemption, progression, connection to heaven, and healing.

THE ATONEMENT OF JESUS CHRIST REDEEMS US FROM SIN AND ERROR

About a month before Christmas in 2018, and in an effort to teach my three-year-old niece, Eliza, about the importance of giving, my mom gave her a small, undecorated Christmas tree of her own. She told Eliza that every time she did something nice for someone else, she could put an ornament on the tree. Eliza loved the idea, and it was her goal from then on to use up all the ornaments provided to her.

Shortly after that, I had the opportunity to take Eliza with me to an art exhibit about the life and ministry of Jesus Christ. The exhibition featured many sculptures and images depicting scenes from His magnificent life. It seemed like a daunting task, trying to entertain a young toddler during such an event while also encouraging her to be reverent. But surprisingly, she loved it.

As we walked amidst the art, I tried to explain to Eliza what Jesus was doing in each of the scenes. In one He was comforting His disciples. In another, healing a blind man. There were stories from His birth all the way until the time of His death and resurrection. Because Jesus Christ spent His ministry doing good things, after looking at each of these sculptures, Liza would turn to me and declare, "That was very nice of Jesus. Do you think He wants to put an ornament on my Christmas tree?"

I wanted so badly to bottle up all of her hope, faith, and innocence. In that moment, I felt so strongly that Heavenly Father knew and loved her. And in an almost indescribable way, I could tell that He was proud of her for making those connections and for taking a seemingly small step toward Him.

I hope you know that He celebrates your small victories too. He is pleased with the improvements you make, no matter how small they appear. Just like little Eliza, we make Heavenly Father proud when we make connections and do good things, even if those things seem inconsequential to us.

As Eliza and I approached one group of sculptures that night, I struggled in my head to know how to tell its accompanying story. It depicted Christ, the woman caught in adultery, and all the people who were accusing her.

How do you explain that story to a three-year-old?

In the end, I told Eliza that this woman made a mistake, and because of that mistake, everyone was mad at her. I told her that Jesus forgave her and encouraged her to be better next time.

For the first time all night, she didn't ask if Jesus wanted to put an ornament on her Christmas tree. Instead, this three-year-old looked at me with complete seriousness in her eyes and whispered, "Livvi, I've made a lot of mistakes."

My heart got caught in my throat as I watched the worry enter her eyes. I wanted to tell her that she was just a little girl and that she wasn't yet accountable for her actions. But instead, I just agreed. "Me too, honey."

"But, Livvi," she continued. "It's okay that we make mistakes sometimes because Jesus forgives us, just like he forgave her." It wasn't a question. It was a statement.

Yes, Eliza. Yes, He does.

We're going to fall short. We're going to make mistakes. We're going to need to repent. Personally, I'm in need of that every single day. And that's not something to be ashamed of or frustrated about. We all do things that we know are wrong. We all say things we don't mean, do things we wish we could erase, and fall so short of being like Jesus.

And of course we do! When we compare ourselves to the only perfect person who has ever lived, we'll fail every single time.

But luckily, He forgives us. He understands us. He wants to help us become better. And with His help, and through His Atonement, we can become all that He wants us to be.

You're never too far gone to be forgiven. There is no limit to the grace that He will offer you. When Christ atoned for the world, that included me and you, as wretched, thoughtless, and unkind as we can be. He atoned for you. He died for you. He paid the price for you to have unlimited chances.

The adversary would have you believe that you *are* too far gone. You *can't* be saved. You're simply *too* rotten to be of any value. But don't buy into that.

Jeffrey R Holland taught, "Only the adversary, the enemy of us all, would try to convince us . . . that people don't really improve, that no one really progresses. And why does Lucifer give that speech? Because he knows he can't improve, he can't progress, that worlds without end he will never have a bright tomorrow. He is a miserable man bound by eternal limitations, and he wants you to be miserable too. Well, don't fall for that. With the gift of the Atonement of Jesus Christ and the strength of heaven to help us, we can improve, and the great thing about the gospel is we get credit for trying, even if we don't always succeed."[1]

Remember when I said that my senior year of high school was a dark and difficult time? I meant that. Tony helped me to solidify my shaking testimony, but that didn't mean I stopped being lonely. It didn't mean that my pain went away or that I suddenly saw sunshine in every circumstance. Things stayed hard. In some ways, they got harder.

One night, during my freshman year of college, I made my way back home after a long day on campus, feeling utterly defeated. My body was continually getting weaker. My grades were slipping almost daily, and I was struggling to maintain a passing score. I didn't have very many friends, and I knew that it was mostly my fault because I never felt well enough to go to social events. I was in survival mode in a lot of areas, and to be completely honest, I had lost all motivation to care. So what if I failed my classes? So what if I stopped going to the doctor? I wasn't getting better anyway, so what was the point in trying?

When I arrived home, I decided to read a talk given by Russell M. Nelson. I don't know why because I certainly wasn't in the mood.

---

1. Jeffrey R. Holland, "Tomorrow the Lord Will Do Wonders among You," April 2016 general conference, https://www.churchofjesuschrist.org/study/general-conference/2016/04/tomorrow-the-lord-will-do-wonders-among-you?lang=eng

But for whatever reason, I found the resolve to read the words in his address, "A Plea to My Sisters."

In this address, President Nelson entreats us to be women of God. He pleads for us to be strong, converted, organized, wise, and steadfast. He talks about needing women who know who they are and where they're going. Women who are courageous and will make the right choices. Women who will speak up and share their voices with the world. He wants women to teach and develop the gift of discernment. Women who know the voice and character of God. Women who trust in His plan for them.

And as I read about these women, I cried because I knew I was not one of them.

There were times I felt strong and courageous. There were days I felt converted. But there were also days that I felt so close to giving up, when I *wanted* to give up. And so I cried because I didn't see how I could ever be a faithful and exemplary woman of God.

I've thought about that night since then. I've thought about how close I was to throwing in the towel and calling it quits. But do you know why I didn't?

Because I was reminded, through the words of Jeffrey R. Holland, that we get credit for trying, even when we don't succeed.

Isn't that the purpose of the Atonement of Jesus Christ? Isn't that the very essence of His grace?

You don't have to suffer for "X" amount of time before asking for help or forgiveness. You don't have to walk a designated section of road alone before you qualify to utilize His Atonement. You qualify simply by being His. The moment you want to change, try to change, or ask for help to change, is the moment His atoning grace will start to heal you.

It may take time. It may take the additional support from your friends, family, and leaders, but if you want to change and be forgiven, you can be. THERE ARE NO EXCEPTIONS TO THAT RULE.

I didn't become the type of woman that President Nelson described overnight. In fact, I'm still trying to become that woman. And it's taken the help, teaching, and examples of many people around me to come as far as I have. It will take the help of many more people to get even closer to that goal. But it *is* possible.

Christ paid the price so that you and I don't have to. In that way, He has already saved us. But we *do* have to accept His offering and offer something of ourselves to Him in return.

But what can we offer Him?

A teachable heart. A changeable life. A desire to be better. Honest efforts to grow and improve, and a willingness to make the changes that He asks us to make.

It doesn't seem like much, but to Him, it's everything.

Don't believe me?

Paul, one of the most famous and steadfast disciples, once lived a life far from the light of the gospel of Jesus Christ. In fact, he once actively persecuted those who did believe and strive to follow our Savior.

He wasn't just someone who fell short or made a few mistakes. He was making efforts to actively fight against what was right. He was, by choice, an enemy to those who *were* trying to do what was right. He was, by choice, an enemy to God.

It would have been easy to label him as "too far gone" or as "damaged goods." To those who had suffered because of his actions, he maybe even seemed unworthy of redemption.

But God saw potential in Saul, as he was then known.

God saw the good that Saul could do.

You can read about it in Acts 9. As Saul journeyed on his way to Damascus, he had a very powerful and profound spiritual experience. He was chastised by Jesus Christ for persecuting the believers, and this shocked and probably scared Saul so much that he committed to change. He asked the Lord what he needed to do to turn his life around.

Jesus gave him instructions to continue into the city where he would receive further information. Although Saul was left blind from that experience and remained blind for three days, he continued on into the city as instructed.

Meanwhile, the Lord spoke to one of his faithful servants, Ananias, in a dream, telling him to go and find Saul, to restore his vision, and to call him to repentance.

The rest of the story is pretty remarkable and is a wonderful example of the redeeming power of Christ's Atonement. Ananias found Saul, blessed him to receive his sight once again, and called him to repentance.

And Saul listened. He changed his name to Paul and was baptized. His heart had completely changed during those days he spent in darkness. And that good that God had seen in him, even in his most wicked moments, really was there. Paul spent the rest of his life devoted to the ministry of the gospel of Jesus Christ.

Isn't it remarkable that Christ could forgive someone so cruel and wicked? Isn't it wonderful to know that Paul wasn't just forgiven, but he was also put to work and used as a wonderful tool in the hands of the Lord?

As much as I love this story, there's another scriptural hero that I look up to even more. His name is Alma the Younger, and his story of repentance is recorded in the Book of Mormon (see Mosiah 26–28, Alma 36).

Alma the Younger was a young man who belonged to a group of people called the Nephites. His father, also named Alma, had been appointed by the king as the Nephites' spiritual leader. The elder Alma was strong in his conviction to the gospel. He truly lived and breathed its teachings.

His son grew up watching his father fulfill righteous callings. He was taught the gospel in his home as well as in his country. Surely he had heard his father's testimony numerous times. And yet, Alma the Younger chose a lifestyle similar to Saul's.

Alma the Younger helped lead a group of unbelievers that mocked, persecuted, and sought to destroy the Church. He turned his back on what he had been taught and on the man who had taught him. He destroyed hearts and testimonies.

And yet, the Lord saw something in him that was worth saving.

Alma the Younger was travelling with four of his friends (who also sought to destroy the Church) when an angel visited them. The angel told them that the elder Alma had been faithfully praying for their redemption and that it was time for Alma the Younger and his friends to change their ways. The event was so powerful and overwhelming that Alma could not speak or move for several days. His friends didn't know how to help him, so they took him home to his father.

When Alma the Younger finally arose again, he had transformed his heart, just as Saul had transformed into Paul. Alma and his friends changed their lives completely and dedicated the rest of their lives to testifying of Jesus Christ, not only among their own people but also among the Lamanites, their enemies.

The reason I love his conversion story, perhaps more than Paul's, is that Alma gives us a lot more detail into what that whole experience felt like for him. During the days in which he couldn't speak or move, Alma the Younger was in agony. He had to confront the sins he had committed and fully recognize the weight and consequences of his wicked actions.

And it nearly killed him.

But in the darkest moments of his despair, he opened his mouth and cried out to the Lord for mercy and forgiveness.

And he received it.

If Christ truly offers love and forgiveness to all who come unto Him, then there's no reason you and I can't have redemption too. But sometimes it is hard. Sometimes it is dark and painful. Sometimes it feels like confronting what we've done is enough to kill us.

But just like Alma the Younger, we can reach out, cry unto the Lord, and be forgiven. "Yea, and as often as my people repent will I forgive them their trespasses against me" (Mosiah 26:30).

The Lord doesn't say that sometimes we will be forgiven, or that we'll be forgiven until we run out of chances. He promises us forgiveness as often as we repent. It's yours to receive as often as you let Him give it to you.

THE ATONEMENT OF JESUS CHRIST ENABLES US TO BECOME BETTER THAN WE ARE NOW

About two thousand years ago, the greatest gift of all was given to the world. Not just a baby, but a chance. Our only hope of returning to our heavenly home. Would you have believed it back then? Could someone so small and innocent really grow up to atone for a world that was in and of itself stripped of innocence? Should He even have to do it?

Surely Mary entertained similar thoughts on occasion. Surely, she prayed for her baby to be safe from any harm or injustice. Surely, she had moments when she didn't want her Son to complete His work. Not because she didn't believe, but because she loved Him more than anything. And when you love someone more than anything, it hurts to watch them suffer, even when you know that suffering is necessary.

But He did grow up. He did atone for an ungrateful world. He did suffer every possible degree of harm and injustice, even until death. And He did it specifically for you and me.

The Atonement of Jesus Christ is undeniably the most vital gift that has ever been given, but I think that quite often we get it wrong. Yes, Christ atoned so that we can repent. That's incredible and vital for our salvation. But it does precious little for our progression. (Stay with me,

I promise this isn't blasphemy.) I don't want to discredit the redemptive power He offers us. It truly is vital. But Jesus Christ didn't just die to redeem us. He also died to help us become everything that we can possibly be.

Of this enabling power, David A. Bednar said, "Most of us clearly understand that the Atonement is for sinners. I am not so sure, however, that we know and understand that the Atonement is also for saints—for good men and women who are obedient and worthy and conscientious and who are striving to become better and serve more faithfully."[2]

We are creatures of progression. This is why the scriptures so frequently entreat us to "change our hearts" or why Paul implored us to "become new creatures" (2 Corinthians 5:17). through Christ. He didn't come to earth to simply restore us to ground zero when we've fallen short. Yes, He wants to forgive us. He wants to save us from sin. But He also wants to see us become something more. Someone more like Him.

We are born on this earth, clean and innocent. Each of us is a blank sheet of paper, teeming with untapped potential. And when we sin, we stain our canvas. Our potential becomes limited *while* the stain exists on the page. But Christ can erase those stains. He can help us become that clean, blank page again.

But He wants more for us than a blank sheet of paper. He sees our potential. And His perfectly creative and artistic heart yearns to pick up a brush and paint us into a masterpiece.

So yes, Christ can redeem. It is necessary that He does so. But He can also create, and He longs to help us become all that we can be.

My best friends are my friends not just because we get along well, but also because they challenge me. They encourage me to progress and become more than I am now. They don't accept my excuses, but they show compassion when I fall short. They don't judge me when I mess

2. David A. Bednar, "In the Strength of the Lord," BYU Speeches, October 23, 2001, https://speeches.byu.edu/talks/david-a-bednar/strength-lord/

up, but they lovingly call me out when I'm making bad decisions. When I'm stuck in a situation and am unsure of where to go, they not only ask me what I think is right, but they also encourage me to act on what I *know* to be right.

One of the reasons Jesus Christ has become my best friend is that He does those same things. He encourages me, but He chastises me too. He guides me, but He also expects me to act on what I already know to be right and good. He challenges me to become something more than I am, and His gospel lays the perfect foundation for that change to take place.

One night, while I was half-asleep on the bathroom floor, begging for pain relief, something unexpected happened. I was chastised. It was three in the morning. I was at my lowest point. And yet, God gave me a list of things to work on.

I was annoyed at first, but ultimately, I knew that I needed to make those changes so that I could become better, and health issues didn't need to interfere with that.

Elder Dallin H. Oaks said, "In contrast to the institutions of the world, which teach us to know something, the gospel of Jesus Christ challenges us to become something. It is not even enough for us to be convinced of the gospel; we must act and think so that we are converted by it."[3]

Our Heavenly Parents and Savior want everything for you. They do not see you as small, unimportant, or defined by your past or present mistakes. They see you as magnificent, vital, and with more potential than you can even fathom for yourself. They want you to become all that you can be, and because of that, they have provided the necessary tools to help you get there. Although there are many things that have been provided to help us progress, I'm only going to focus on

---

3. Dallin H. Oaks, "The Challenge to Become," October 2000 general conference, https://www.churchofjesuschrist.org/study/general-conference/2000/10/the-challenge-to-become?lang=eng

three Christlike attributes that have helped me understand the gospel better.

Faith, Hope, and Charity

First faith. Do you believe in Jesus Christ? Do you believe in His gospel? If so, great. Continue believing, continue studying, continue repenting. But if you don't believe, I hope you know that's okay too. One of the great things about our Savior is that He meets us where we are right now and walks with us the entire way home. The only thing He requires of you is a willing heart. And that includes any heart that's unsure but still willing to believe in Him.

I've watched from the sidelines as people completely change their lives. I've seen broken individuals become whole. I've seen angry hearts become meek and humble. I've seen vastly different individuals embrace one another as brothers and sisters in God's kingdom. And what connected all of these miraculous events? What thread of commonality was interwoven throughout each of these moments? It was not any particular denomination. Instead, it was Him.

Jesus Christ has this miraculous ability to see the good in people, regardless of their background or circumstances. He, simply because His nature is one of love, draws out the very best in people. He turns our weaknesses into strengths and our strengths into service opportunities. He shows us not only how similar you and I are to each other, but also how similar we are to Him. While the adversary tries to hide those similarities and highlight all of the ways in which we are so different and far from Christ, our Savior chooses to celebrate the ways in which we *are* becoming like Him. He never asks us to be perfect on our own. Instead, He asks us to let Him perfect us.

So start small. Pray for even the smallest desire to believe. Start studying the scriptures with an open mind. Begin asking questions with the intent of receiving honest answers. If you do that, and continue to do that even when it's hard, I promise that faith will come.

As we discover and strengthen our faith, we need to have hope. Thomas S. Monson entreated us to "be of good cheer. [Because] the future is as bright as [our] faith."[4] Do we believe that? Do we believe that God has something bigger and brighter waiting for us up ahead?

At times I didn't believe that things would get better. When I was in the midst of one of the lowest and darkest moments of my life, I was sure that no light was strong enough to illuminate my way. Nothing could possibly shine bright enough to lead me to higher ground.

My friends, I have never been happier to admit that I was wrong.

There was light and hope available to me, and there is peace, joy, and happiness waiting for you. If you are suffering in the garden and you're convinced you're all alone, I assure you that you're not. To borrow the words of Jeffrey R. Holland,

"Even if you cannot always see that silver lining on your clouds, God can, for He is the very source of the light you seek. He does love you, and He knows your fears. He hears your prayers. He is your Heavenly Father, and surely, He matches with His own the tears His children shed. [So] don't you quit. You keep walking. You keep trying. There is help and happiness ahead. Some blessings come soon, some come late, and some don't come until heaven; but for those who embrace the gospel of Jesus Christ, they come. It will be all right in the end. Trust God and believe in good things to come."[5]

I think about Mary, the mother of Christ, often. I cannot imagine how someone so strong and selfless could have existed. It's not surprising to me that God chose her to bring His Son into the world. She must have been a shining example of both faith and hope.

---

4. Thomas S. Monson, "Be of Good Cheer," April 2009 general conference, https://www.churchofjesuschrist.org/study/general-conference/2009/04/be-of-good-cheer?lang=eng
5. Jeffrey R. Holland, "An High Priest of Good Things to Come,"Ensign, November 1999, https://www.churchofjesuschrist.org/study/ensign/1999/11/an-high-priest-of-good-things-to-come?lang=eng

Think about it. How could she possibly have had the courage to tell Joseph that she was pregnant unless she had faith that God would soften his heart and deliver her? How could she have withstood the pressures of parenting the very Son of God, unless she trusted that God would multiply her efforts, magnify her strengths, and make up for her shortcomings? How could she have watched Him die on the cross unless she had faith and hope that He would rise again and return to her?

I used to have a hard time understanding the difference between faith and hope. Both, it seemed, required a belief in God. Both, it seemed, necessitated some measure of trust on our part. But what else? And in what ways are they different?

I think that faith is trusting in God. It's believing that He is there and that He has a plan. But I think hope is believing that our lives will be better and happier because of that plan. Let me give you an example.

When I was sick, really sick, I didn't live like everyone else. I didn't live at all. I just survived.

I remember one summer, when I was fourteen or so, that was particularly difficult. My body rejected everything I gave it. There wasn't a food or drink that I could tolerate. Even water triggered an intense pain that left me crumpled on the floor for hours.

At some point I stopped eating, not because I didn't want to but because I was terrified of the pain returning. Instead, I drank water and meal-replacement shakes, but only as often as necessary to keep me out of the hospital, for they, too, brought pain with them. I often went days between real meals, and even then, I only ate because my parents begged me to.

I wonder now how I survived that particular summer. Physically I was barely hanging on. But emotionally? How did I possibly suffer through it?

It was entirely faith and hope.

That may sound cliché, but I absolutely mean it. At this point, I had accepted that I was a daughter of God. I knew He was listening to me. I knew He was aware of me. And I knew He had a plan for me. But the real reason I was able to hang on was that I knew that my life would ultimately be better because of His plan.

My faith told me that there was a reason for my pain. I would learn from it. I would grow from it. My faith taught me that I was accounted for. God knew about my illness; it wasn't something that surprised Him or slipped through the cracks. He was absolutely prepared to help me through my pain.

My hope, however, taught me that I wouldn't always be in pain. Even if it wasn't until the next life, my body *would* be made whole. My hope told me that my life would be better for having endured such a trial. *I* would be better for it. My hope taught me that every moment I spent faithfully enduring would be made right and that the blessings ultimately would outweigh the pain.

So, faith teaches us to trust in God's plan. And hope encourages us to believe that His plan is best. But both are found in Christ, for it is Christ who is central to God's plan. And it is Christ who gives birth to every happy ending and positive outcome.

The third aspect, charity, is often the easiest to define, but the hardest to put into practice. It comes to most of us fairly naturally around the Christmas season. It seems that everywhere you look people are serving and loving strangers, in some small effort to honor the one person who defined what charity should be. But when the Christmas season ends, it's much harder to love without reservation. It is hard to love your roommates when they leave their dishes in the sink for days, especially after you've kindly asked them to clean up. It is hard to love the person who cut you off on the interstate, or to serve someone who always seems to take too much without giving anything in return. It is difficult to have patience and to be kind.

But if we are to ever become half as good as He is, we must learn to love half as well as He does.

So how do we begin to love as the Lord did?

I had an experience when I was younger that changed how I approach service and charitable acts.

I was attending a youth conference in the summer, and honestly, I couldn't tell you what the theme was. I don't remember what book of scripture we were studying or any of the activities that we did. All I remember is the moment that taught me to love people a little more generously.

I began this youth conference with an earnest desire to receive spiritual edification. Again, this was in the beginning years of my illness. I needed encouragement and strength more than I had ever needed it before. But I was distracted. Not just during one of the devotionals either. I was distracted almost constantly by one of the other girls in our group.

It wasn't that I didn't get along with her per se; it's just that I didn't want to be around her. She was younger than me, louder than me, and constantly interrupting everyone who tried to tell a story, bear their testimony, or make an announcement. It drove me nuts.

How could I possibly learn anything or strengthen my testimony when she was turning the whole experience into a joke?

I remember praying before going to bed on our second to last night, venting to God about how all I wanted was to have a good experience and grow my testimony. But how could I do that when I was always around someone who clearly didn't want to be there? I spent a great deal of time complaining about her to God.

At some point during this prayer, I realized that I had hardened my heart against her so much that I'd closed myself off to the Spirit, too. The reason I wasn't learning anything at this conference was because of me, not because of her. I put the wall up. And even though I thought I was building it between her and me, I was building it between the Spirit and me too. And that makes sense, because the Spirit can't reside where there is contention, even if that contention is one-sided and even when it isn't directed toward heaven.

Once I recognized the walls I had built for what they were, I immediately wished I could take them down. But how? She didn't even know I was angry with her. It wasn't her heart that needed to be healed; it was mine. So how could I fix that?

I prayed for a long time. Eventually I decided that the only way to tear down a wall built from hate was with tools made from love. So, I prayed and prayed that my eyes could be opened and that I could see her as our Heavenly Father does. I just wanted a glimpse of the love He had for her so that I could borrow some of it and love her too.

The next morning, I sat at a picnic table quietly eating my breakfast. She was at another table, but I could see her from where I sat. *Please,* I silently prayed. *Please help me.*

I glanced up at her again in between bites, but I had a hard time looking away for several long moments because she suddenly looked different. I'm not exactly sure what changed in that moment, or how to describe what I experienced. It was almost like I caught a glimpse of her potential; a small view of what God must see in her. She seemed to me to be surrounded by light, but I couldn't tell if it originated from around or inside of her. Either way, she was radiant and good and *divine.* I felt almost overwhelmed by the warmth and love that I suddenly felt for her, and I knew that it was merely a fraction of how much God really loves her. It was entirely awe-inspiring and humbling.

We never became best friends, although I wish I could say that I had been able to do that. Instead, I just reflected on that experience any time I noticed myself building that wall of judgment again. I remembered the love God has for her and borrowed some of it to keep that wall from ever building all the way back up. That experience has caused me to stop and reflect on my thoughts and actions toward other people on numerous occasions.

Although I'm so far from perfect when it comes to loving people like our Savior did, I learned something incredible from that experience.

God wants us to love one another. He wants it so much, in fact, that it's second only to the commandment to love Him. And because He wants us to love one another, He's willing to teach us how to love, show us how to love, and, if necessary, loan out some of His love from time to time until we can create some of our own.

He will show you how to love your neighbor, estranged father, or nagging client that never seems to thank you for the work you do. He can teach you how to love them in the way that they need and want to be loved. He will freely give you direction on how to serve those you minister to or how to rebuild a broken relationship. You just have to ask Him, with a sincere heart and an honest commitment to do what He instructs, and to make the changes that He asks you to make.

Maybe you won't see a light, have your breath taken away from an overwhelming amount of love, or feel at a loss for words. But you might find yourself inspired to write someone a note, buy cookies for the homeless man sitting on the street corner, or hold your tongue when you feel like criticizing. You might have a little extra patience on a day when someone really needs you to be patient with them. You might be blessed with a little more financial flexibility than normal to donate to your favorite charitable fund or to a family that's in need. You might walk into your Sunday meetings and find that the only available seat is next to the woman who always sits alone.

God provides opportunities for us to love His children, and as we consistently pray for those opportunities and for a measure of His love and perspective, we can begin to act in faith, hope, and charity.

So, with these three attributes as our catalysts for change, let's get to work. Set honest, righteous goals for yourself. Decide today whom you want to be a year from now, a month from now, or even a week from now. Pick one thing to work on *today* and keep yourself accountable to the Lord. Tell Him about your progress. Ask for help when you're falling short. Allow Him to share in both your failures and your victories, no matter how miniscule they seem.

One thing I've realized is that whether I'm working toward earning a degree or wanting to improve a relationship with a family member, God cares. He cares about my progress as a whole. He cares when I set goals, and He wants to help me succeed in them. He wants to help you succeed in all of your ambitions, too.

Still speaking of the enabling power of Christ's Atonement, David A. Bednar continued, "Individual willpower, personal determination and motivation, and effective planning and goal setting are necessary but ultimately insufficient to triumphantly complete this mortal journey. Truly we must come to rely upon 'the merits, and mercy, and grace of the Holy Messiah' (2 Nephi 2:8)."[6]

I mentioned this a bit earlier, but I'll say it again because it's worth stating twice. I think that some of us mistakenly believe that we have to put in a certain amount of work entirely on our own in order to be forgiven, to receive strength, or to have Christ involved in our lives. And while it is important to walk by faith and actively do our part, we were never asked to do it alone.

You don't need to carry your cross without help.

It is noble that you want to do your part, but don't mistakenly believe that you'll somehow earn your salvation. You'll never earn it, but you can still have it. Heaven cheers you on when you put forth efforts to come unto Christ, because it's through Christ that you'll return to heaven.

So take your willpower, determination, and planning and give it to Christ. Decide to choose Him. Stay determined to represent Him. Plan on letting Him lead, and you'll go further than you ever could have on your own.

THE ATONEMENT OF JESUS CHRIST CONNECTS US TO HEAVEN

Last year I sat in the back of our church building with my roommates. In the front of the room hung a portrait of Christ kneeling in the Garden of Gethsemane. It was Frans Schwartz's *Agony in the Garden*,

6. Bednar, "In the Strength of the Lord."

one of my favorite renditions of this scene, and one that now hangs on my apartment wall. Our teacher asked us to look at the painting and share our thoughts on it. Most people focused on His facial expressions or the coloring that Schwartz used to paint this scene. Only one answer focused on what Christ was actually doing in the painting.

"He's praying," my roommate noted quietly. "Isn't it amazing that we get to communicate with God in the exact same way that Christ communicated with Him? Prayer is universal. It's for everyone."

I've thought about that often since then because she was right. It is amazing that we get to communicate with God in the same way that Christ did. It's amazing to think that prayer is for both the sinner and the saint. It is almost overwhelming to know that we have access to heaven in the exact same way that our Savior, the Son of God, did.

This is one aspect of Christ's Atonement that I often forget to attribute to Him, which is silly because it's the one resulting effect of His sacrifice that I use more than anything else. I pray daily, sometimes even constantly, but I often forget that prayer is yet another gift from our Savior.

The Atonement of Jesus Christ connects us to heaven. Quite literally, and not just in moments when we're on our knees talking to God. Think about all the things that connect us to heaven: prayers, priesthood blessings, ordinances, and covenants. All of those things are done in the name of Jesus Christ because He is our link between heaven and earth.

He's our link between everything.

Life and death.

Godly and ungodly.

Sin and salvation.

In between it all, it is Christ.

It's easy to forget that those moments of revelation and quiet connections to heaven resulted directly from Christ's willingness to be our mediator. After all, in those moments we aren't standing face to face with our Savior. Instead, we're face to face, or maybe spirit to spirit, with the Holy Ghost.

I think that sometimes we undervalue the gift that the constant presence of the Spirit truly is. Not intentionally, of course, but we still do it.

When you walk into a grocery store, you don't consciously think, "Oh look! The lights are on!" The thought never even crosses your mind because, well, of course the lights would be on. You expect them to be. How else would all the customers see the products that they need to buy?

You don't consciously notice the light because you're used to it. But you would notice its absence immediately. Imagine it. If you walked into that grocery store and it was completely dark, your first thoughts would probably be, "Something is wrong. Why are the lights turned off?"

Sometimes we do that with our spirituality too. We don't consciously notice the influence of the Holy Ghost until we're suddenly living without it. But we should strive to be conscious of the Spirit's influence because it does so much good for our lives.

The Holy Ghost works hand in hand with God and with Jesus Christ. They are of one heart and of one mind, and they are one in purpose too. That purpose is to help bring us home.

Think about it. Christ's Atonement was infinite, which means that it was complete in every way. He suffered for our sins so that we don't have to be condemned by them. He experienced death so that He could overcome it and in turn allow us to do the same. But He also experienced pain, heartbreak, and sorrow so that He could understand and support us. He experienced our joys and successes exactly as we have so that He could celebrate with us. He experienced your unique set of suffocations and celebrations so that He could know you and understand your heart completely.

He knows what motivates you, what tempts and hurts you. He knows the reasons you're afraid, and He cheers for you when you're strong and brave. Simply put, He knows all the things that make you, *you.*

And because He knows you, He knows your unique needs, and He sends the Holy Ghost, His messenger, to fulfill those needs. This means that because of the Atonement of Jesus Christ, you can be connected to heaven in times of success as well as in times of failure.

It's honestly terrifying to me to imagine a world without connection to heaven. I cannot see how anyone can have hope or faith for the future without some divine direction or encouragement. It's a reality that I can't think about for very long because I know how utterly lost I would be. I'm so grateful to live in this world with God's plan, allowing us to have access to heaven as often as we need it.

I guess that's one thing I never expected when I first got sick. I figured I would learn something about God, and I did. I learned that He's truly my Father and that, like any good parent, He truly cares about my welfare. It hurts Him to see me in pain. It brings Him joy to see me grow from the challenges I'm facing. But He's cheering me on and anxiously waiting for my return home.

I also figured I would learn something about Jesus Christ, and again, I did. He's different from my Heavenly Father, though. My relationship with Him feels different too. I don't think Jesus Christ is waiting for me at heaven's gate. Instead, it feels like He's here with me now, helping me navigate my way home. He's suffering through things with me, allowing me to go out and have this growing experience on Earth, while still ensuring that I can come home, if that's what I choose.

But the one thing I didn't anticipate as a result of my sickness was the personal relationship I would develop with that third member of the Godhead, the Holy Ghost. This relationship is once again different from the other two but still just as valuable and distinct. I've learned how the Spirit communicates with me, what type of environment that Spirit prefers, and how I can be a better host. Even though it is Jesus Christ that connects us to heaven, it's often through His Holy Spirit that that connection is manifested.

So let's talk about the Holy Ghost for a minute. Most of what I know is about the Spirit's role and character.

The Spirit does God's work, which means that like Jesus Christ, the Holy Ghost goes about doing good, directing us toward heaven, and brings messages of love and peace to us from heaven. Although there are many things that the Spirit does, there are three things that I think are pretty universal.

PEACE AND COMFORT

The most common prayer for peace that I hear is after someone has passed away. We pray for comfort and for strength to endure the physical and emotional pain that the loss of a loved one can bring. In short, we often ask for peace when it is accompanied by death. I guess it makes sense when you think about it. I'm twenty-three years old and I've been to at least twenty funerals. Crazy, huh? I've seen lots of friends, family members, and neighbors pass away. And one thing I've realized over the years is that it never gets easier. It never stops hurting. You never stop missing them.

Yes, you learn to keep going. Yes, you learn to let life go on. But that doesn't mean you love or miss the person any less. You've just learned to survive their absence.

But death is not the only circumstance that may have us crying out for help. Christ's Atonement brings the Holy Ghost more abundantly into our lives, and that means we can receive peace, strength, comfort, or direction in any number of circumstances. In fact, according to the sacramental prayers, we can receive those gifts of the spirit always.

Christ knows how your heart shattered when your spouse declared their desire for a divorce. He knows how badly you wanted to die with the loss of your young child. He knows how sincerely you want to get married, have children, or find steady employment. He knows how hard you're trying to be brave. He knows how often you fall short. He knows you're not perfect, and how there are some days when you don't even want to try to be. He sees your little efforts. He feels your honest prayers. He is with you, even when you want to disappear from this world. And He is with you, even when our prayers aren't answered in the ways we hoped that they would be.

I used to think that if I had enough faith in my Savior, He would just take my hardships away. My grandparents wouldn't pass away because God would make them get better. My pain wouldn't be here to stay because He'd give my doctors the answers we needed. I wouldn't have to worry about losing friends or struggling with depression because the Light of Christ would shine brightly enough to make all the gray disappear.

But guess what? It never disappeared. It's still there most of the time.

My grandparents didn't get better. My doctors didn't receive answers. Many of my friends walked away. And the darkness and loneliness of mental health struggles still push back at me, making it hard to get out of bed some days.

Christ is fighting beside us, not in place of us. We still have to don our armor and defend the front lines. We're still doing the work. The difference is that we're no longer defending those lines alone. With Him, the war is already won. The outcome already assured in our favor. But the battle continues on for a while longer.

The good news is that He is with us.

And so is His Spirit.

Amid every heartbreak and moment of hopelessness, I felt the comforting companionship of the Spirit. It didn't make my heart whole again or suddenly give me motivation to rise up and continue on. Most of the time my hard days stay hard. But the companionship of the Holy Ghost reminds me that even when I'm broken, I'm heard. Even when I'm lonely, I'm accompanied by heaven. In my experience, this does little to make things instantly "better," but it does a whole lot to keep you holding on from moment to moment.

Peace. Comfort. Reassurance. Although seemingly small and almost unhelpful at times, these gifts of the Spirit slowly bring increased light and happiness into our lives, even if it takes years for us to notice.

PERSONAL REVELATION

I used to worry that my prolonged health issues remained mysterious and untreatable because I had done something wrong. I had somehow offended heaven, or maybe God specifically, and now I was paying for it. It was only fair, after all. If I wasn't repenting for whatever way I had mocked heaven, then surely God had every right to punish me.

The problem was that I honestly couldn't think of what I had done to suffer so greatly.

I'm not insinuating that I'm perfect, completely innocent, and entirely undeserving of corrections. On the contrary, I desperately need chastisement, even continual chastisement. I am far from perfect, but I do make an active effort to repent once I've recognized my mistakes.

In this case, however, I honestly couldn't figure out what I had done at age ten to bring on the wrath of God by age eleven.

This has bothered me for most of the last decade, although I never admitted it aloud. I never told anyone how wretchedly guilty I felt for causing my parents worry and financial stress. I never confessed how sometimes, when my doctors remained confused about my symptoms and when yet another test result proclaimed I was healthy when I clearly wasn't, I felt like God was punishing me for something. Rationally, I knew this was most likely not the case. I believe that *had* God been punishing me, He would have at least indicated how I had sinned. So yes, rationally, I knew that this was not an act of Godly vengeance.

But pain makes people irrational.

In January of 2019, I fought with this thought process once again and asked God the question that I had been asking for so many years now. Why was I sick?

This time, a response pressed itself very firmly in my head.

"You are not ill because you have sinned. You are ill so that God can showcase His work unto man."

I cannot begin to describe the relief I felt at those words. Even if it had no effect on my physical health, it was critical for improving my emotional health. I no longer had to feel guilty. I no longer had to wonder if I had made God angry. I could be at peace emotionally, even if I was still sick physically.

Sometimes revelation from heaven is for our own benefit, aiding us in making a decision or allowing us to let go of emotional pain. But sometimes revelation from heaven is for the benefit of others, in the form of a prompting to serve.

Occasionally, we hear miraculous stories of people receiving very specific promptings that end up changing their lives. One day your neighbor cancels their plans in order to visit a long-lost relative, only to discover that relative in the hospital, in dire need of cookies and company. Okay, I'm being hyperbolic here and I shouldn't be. Those kinds of promptings *are* real. Those opportunities to serve do present themselves. But for every big prompting that someone feels, there are a hundred other smaller promptings too.

Thomas S. Monson once declared that we should never postpone promptings. He encouraged us to act on them immediately.

I don't know about you, but that seemed very daunting to me. I've never been good at knowing what a prompting of the Spirit was and what was just from my own head, so when it came to acting on promptings, I very definitely postponed them. I worried about them. I prayed to know how to tell the difference between inspiration and my own thoughts. And by the time I acted, I was often too late.

It wasn't until yet another conversation with Tony that I felt a little clarity. He told me that it didn't really matter if the ideas in my head were divinely inspired or not, so long as they were good.

"Let's say they aren't promptings. They're good ideas but not sent from heaven. What's the harm in acting on them? Is there any harm? At minimum, you've shown someone you were thinking about them. At most, you were an answer to their prayers."

Once again, Tony changed my perspective. I could have argued that it would be *nice* to know which thoughts are real promptings and that sometimes acting on promptings can be kind of scary, but he would have just shrugged and told me that growth didn't come from comfort zones.

Another lesson I learned: Grown-ups can be so annoyingly right sometimes.

I didn't act on his advice for a while because, again, reaching out to people without knowing it was the right thing to do could be kind of scary. Truthfully, it can be scary even when you do know that it's the right thing to do. But eventually, almost two years later, I decided to give Tony's philosophy a shot.

Honestly, it was annoying at first.

Every time I had a thought to reach out to someone or to stop and talk to someone who was sitting alone, I wanted to reject it. I didn't want to put myself out there. But slowly, I did. I didn't act on every thought at first, and I still took my time responding. Sometimes the people I reached out to responded with gratitude. Sometimes they didn't respond at all.

But their response didn't matter so much because as I acted, I realized that there was goodness in that. I felt better somehow by complimenting a stranger on their shoes or by buying a meal for the next person in line. It helped me not be so focused on myself.

Over time I've made more efforts to respond to those thoughts faster and more eagerly. And the more I act on these spiritual promptings, or maybe just good thoughts, the more of them I seem to have. I still have trouble distinguishing between them sometimes. I still can't always tell which ones are divinely inspired. But I learned that if you're willing to serve, God will give you opportunities, or at least help you to be aware of the opportunities that already exist.

Tony was right. It didn't do any harm to act on a good thought.

CONFIRMATION OF TRUTH

The third main way that I've felt the Spirit influence my life is through testimony. The testimony of the Holy Ghost.

That's one of the many important roles of the Holy Ghost: to bear testimony of things that are right. I think this will feel different for everyone, but personally, I feel a small warmth in my chest that grows until I feel happy and grateful. Maybe this sounds odd, but it's almost as if my own spirit is agreeing. When the Holy Ghost confirms something to me, I can feel it resonate inside me. It just feels true. I'll give you a couple of examples of this.

One year, during my days in a church youth program, our leaders challenged each of us to memorize "The Living Christ," a document that testifies of Jesus Christ, His life, and His ministry.

I had never even read this document before I decided to accept their challenge and memorize it. I didn't know much about it at the time. But when I began to read through it that first night, I felt something small stir in my heart. And each subsequent time I read it, that little feeling grew. When I finally memorized it in its entirety, it was hard not to get emotional reciting the words.

The Spirit had confirmed its truthfulness to me over those weeks, and my own testimony of Jesus Christ has been strengthened because of it.

In a more recent experience, I felt the Spirit confirm the truthfulness of this gospel again, this time in a matter of moments rather than over the course of many weeks.

I was entering a Latter-day Saint temple for the first time to make covenants with the Lord.

Deciding to go to the temple had been a difficult and prayerful process for me. I had always planned on going, but growing up, I had imagined that I would make those covenants shortly before getting married or serving a mission to proclaim my testimony to the world. I never imagined that I would go through at twenty years old for no other reason than because I wanted to be there with Him. I wanted to be in His house and make those covenants. I felt spiritually ready to do so.

So I contacted my bishop and did my best to prepare myself spiritually. When the day came for me to receive my endowment, I was shocked at how happy, peaceful, and at home I felt inside the temple walls. With my family beside me, I felt more confident and hopeful than I had ever felt before.

Hours later, when I was back at my apartment and all alone, I found myself wondering if my deceased grandparents were proud of me and wishing that they could have been there with me. I thought about the testimonies of my grandparents. They hadn't always verbally testified of Christ, but I knew from the way they lived that they loved the Lord and believed in Him. I knew that if He was proud of me, then they would be too.

As I lay on the couch, staring at the ceiling, I verbalized my thoughts.

"Heavenly Father," I began softly, "are you proud of me?"

The warmth of the Spirit flooded through my chest in a firm and resounding yes.

What I needed in that moment (and honestly every moment since) was the confirmation that I was (and am) on the right path. The Spirit whispers these truths to me, corrects me when I'm wrong, and helps me to feel God's love.

THE ATONEMENT OF JESUS CHRIST HAS THE POWER TO HEAL US

Most people who believe in Jesus Christ agree that He has the power to make you and I whole. Like we discussed in the beginning, He is a healer. Broken? He'll fix you. Burdened? He'll raise you up. Blind? He can help you see.

That's why the accounts of Him healing beggars and performing miracles are declared so frequently. We resonate with those broken people. We see ourselves in them and receive the encouragement we need to seek healing through Christ despite our limitations.

But I think sometimes, as we focus on the Atonement of Jesus Christ, we only highlight the ways in which He can spiritually heal us. Important, yes. But let's not forget that an infinite Atonement gave way for immeasurable healing. We can be healed spiritually, emotionally, physically, and in any other way you can think of. An infinite Atonement equals opportunities for holistic growth and healing.

Emotional Healing

Sometimes I look at the people around me and wonder how anyone is surviving, let alone being kind and generous and Christlike. Perhaps that's a bit cynical of me, but it's true. There's just so much pain and heartache in the lives of the people around me, and I cannot comprehend how anyone is holding on as well as they are. Maybe you all are just a lot stronger than I am.

I've watched parents bury their young children, and young children bury their parents. I've seen individuals abandon Christ, not because they didn't believe but because of the bullying that they experienced at the hands of people who called themselves friends.

I've watched families torn apart from death, divorce, or disownment. I've seen some of the most faithful disciples slowly lose their light as they continued down cold and lonely paths, only to end up lost in the dark, wondering why God wasn't answering their prayers.

I've also witnessed people from all around the world cling to the smallest tendrils of faith left in them, until finally they could acquire just a little bit more. I've seen people refined and sculpted by their trials. I've seen others flattened and destroyed by them.

I cannot judge either reaction. I've reacted in both ways at different times in my life, but I think that one of the hardest parts of both enduring and understanding these kinds of situations is confronting the emotional pain that it leaves you with.

A good friend of mine recently reached out to me, confiding in me about a very difficult trial she was going through. She told me that although she felt optimistic about the future, she couldn't shake the emotional pain of feeling completely alone. And there was fear, too. Fear that she was abandoned and that maybe it was better that way. She wondered if being alone somehow meant that she was unlovable.

I want you to imagine that your friend or family member posed that same question to you. They come to you and quietly confess their worst fear. They are unlovable. They are unworthy. They are alone and it's better off that way.

I'm sure that most of us would be quick to reassure them of their worth and importance. We'd dispel those fears if we could because of course being alone doesn't make you less loved.

And yet, that's still a very *valid* feeling and a very *understandable* worry. It's also relatable. I think most of us have felt similarly at some point in our lives, and if you haven't, I'm sorry to say that you probably will.

So as this beautiful and brave friend of mine questioned her worth, I thought about how I could best respond. I didn't want to discredit her feelings by informing her that her math was wrong, that she was jumping to conclusions, and that her fears weren't anything to worry about. Because however inaccurate they were, they were still real to her. So instead, I sat thoughtfully for a few minutes as I prayed for guidance on what to say. This is what I finally responded with:

"The presence of other people does not determine how lovable or worthy of love you are. Jesus Christ was betrayed by His friends. He walked the loneliest of paths. And He died while people looked on and cheered.

"But He was still worthy of love. In fact, He was more worthy of love than the rest of us.

"He was still loved. He was still lovable. And yet, He was alone.

"You, likewise, are still loved. You are also still worthy and deserving of that love. The presence of other people will not change that.

"I know it feels like maybe you're broken or damaged, and like maybe you won't have that love again. I know it feels like it might stay this way forever, but it won't. You won't always be alone. You aren't even alone now, although I understand completely why it feels that way. But this feeling won't last forever. I promise."

When we're forced to face emotional pain, it can feel like it's the end. And as much as the people around you might try to help, they'll probably end up saying some stupid, hurtful, and quite frankly, insensitive things. These people aren't perfect, and sadly, you'll have to deal with the consequences of their actions. But there will also be people who will stand by you, even when they cannot offer help.

Think about the women in Christ's life for a moment. Mary, His mother, and Mary Magdalene, among others, were some of the only people who stood by Him constantly. When He was crucified, they stood at the foot of the cross and cried with Him and for Him. They couldn't help Him at that point. In fact, during much of His persecution they were unable to help Him. But they could stay near Him, silently sustaining Him.

And so they did. In life, at death, and even after He had been laid in the tomb, these faithful women stayed close to their Savior, refusing to deny or forsake Him. It was all they could offer—not even comfort or words of encouragement, just their constant presence and quiet love.

Just as Christ had these faithful loved ones near Him, you too will have others to bear you up. Maybe they're friends, family, or other believers in Christ around the world that you've never had the chance to meet. Or maybe you'll have none of those people and you'll feel entirely and utterly alone.

But I testify to you that when *you're* nailed to the cross and people are cheering and applauding *your* pain, Jesus Christ, like His own mother was, will be standing there, quietly sustaining you.

I'm going to add my strength and voice to His (as small as it may be in comparison) and tell you that in life, in death, and everything in between and afterward, you will not be left alone. You will not be unloved or unsustained by Him. Not for a second.

Physical Healing

I spent years utterly fascinated with the accounts of Christ healing the sick and afflicted. I used to imagine what it would have been like to feel His hands rest upon my head and to receive a blessing from Him. I told myself that had I been privileged to walk with my Savior, I would have been faithful enough to receive His healing too.

So I guess it wasn't really a surprise that when I first developed health issues, the little eleven-year-old brain in my head never considered that I might not actually get better. It never occurred to me that this illness might last or that God might not heal me.

God *not* healing me had never been an option to consider. Of course, He would heal me. I was absolutely sure that He had the power to do so, so I never even considered an alternative.

In the beginning of my 'sick days,' I used to imagine what it would be like to be healed. I assumed that it would come through a priesthood blessing from my dad, maybe the bishop, or maybe even someone like the prophet. Surely God could tell him where to find me.

They would rest their hands upon my head and invoke the power of God to heal me. And that would be it. I would stand up and walk away whole.

Shockingly, this was not the case.

Those first few months of being sick were difficult for me, particularly emotionally. I didn't understand how to manage chronic pain. To make matters worse, my doctors had no idea what was even wrong with me, so they couldn't provide the guidance I needed. I thought doctors were supposed to have all the answers. I never anticipated that my case would have them scratching their heads in confusion.

One thing that nobody tells you is that it's okay to be upset with God. It's okay to cry out to Him in anger and frustration. It's okay to blame Him for something in a moment of heartbreak. It's okay to yell and cry and scream. In fact, I think it's probably healthy. The key is to not give up on Him.

I spent two or three months unbelievably angry with Him for making me sick, or for at least allowing me to remain so. But eventually the anger became too exhausting, and I only had two options left: forgive God or walk away.

Again, the key is to not give up on Him, so I chose the forgiveness route. Now I realize that He hadn't done anything wrong, but in the moment, it felt like an enormous act of faith to choose to trust Him. And maybe it was a big act of faith at the time.

For the first time in my life, I considered what I would do if healing never came to me in this life. That was HARD. It's unbelievably difficult to force yourself to consider a lifetime of that much pain as a potential reality. I wrestled with that for a long, long time. It took a lot of study and getting to know Christ before I could comfortably say that I trusted God enough to stay sick.

Years of pain. Years of heartache. Years of hoping. Years of submitting. Years of feeling that hope repeatedly shatter. And six long years before I finally heard the words I had been longing to hear.

"The Lord wants you to know that healing is coming, and it's coming soon."

It's hard to describe the feeling that accompanied those words. I don't even remember who was giving me that particular priesthood blessing. I only remember the words.

I felt like new life had been breathed into me.

Healing was coming, and soon! I felt giddy and motivated. I remember the thoughts that raced through my head. *God is going to heal me. He's finally going to do it. This is almost over.* My thoughts turned to prayers. *Oh, Heavenly Father, thank you! I promise I'll do whatever you ask me to. Guide me to the right doctors and treatments and I'll do what they tell me to,* whatever *they tell me to do.*

I guess I had realized somewhere along the road that *if* God chose to heal me, He would probably do so through modern medicine. After all, that knowledge was inspired, and I fully believe that God expects us to use all the resources that He has given us.

Fast forward over three years, six more doctors, and three surgeries later. I was exhausted. I'd had several priesthood blessings since that pivotal moment, and many of them had said the same thing, almost word for word.

"The Lord wants you to know that healing is coming, and it's coming soon."

I still believed it, but wow—God and I apparently had very different definitions of the word *soon*. I had exhausted my options, hadn't I? I had tried everything that every doctor I'd seen could think of. Every diet. Every medication. Every surgery, procedure, and treatment. I'd even tried some lesser known, eastern medicine techniques. Everything helped for a few weeks, but nothing seemed to last. As far as my doctors could tell, they had fixed every problem, patched up every hole, and reset every circuit. All that was left was for my body to recover, to heal from all the trauma it had sustained over the years.

But it wouldn't do that. For whatever reason, my body didn't seem to want to heal. The processes that were meant to restore and revitalize the body just wouldn't kick into gear. And my doctors had no explanation for that.

I remember that night quite clearly, the night when things finally changed for me. It was February 26, 2019, at one or two in the morning.

It had been a rough week for me. My new treatments were making me far sicker than normal, but I was sticking with them, fueled by the hope that endurance would eventually pay off. My immune system was weak, and I had concocted a bad combination of strep throat and the flu. I hadn't left my bed for days except to visit the emergency room for a few hours with intense kidney and (mock) appendix pain.

I was dehydrated. I was exhausted. And to top it all off, my nose had been bleeding on and off for the last twenty-four hours. (Way to kick somebody while they're down, huh?)

So there I was, awake in the earliest hours of the day, nursing yet *another* bloody nose and wishing I could just get some rest.

The room was very still, even for the late hour. I remember noticing how uncommonly quiet it was. I looked over at my roommate, but she was fast asleep.

I wasn't planning on praying, meaning that I wasn't kneeling or folding my arms. In fact, my eyes were open, staring at the far wall, and drifting lazily around the room as one hand held a wad of tissues to my face.

"Heavenly Father," I began meekly. "I'm exhausted. I'm not strong enough to heal from one thing, let alone all of these things at once."

I began to get emotional and angry, though I kept my voice quiet to avoid waking my roommate. "You told me over three years ago that healing was coming. You promised, and I believed you. I did what you asked. I did everything the doctors asked, too. I don't have any other options to explore. I don't have anything left to give."

I paused. I'm not sure why, but I remember thinking, *Why do you think God will heal you with medicine?*

That question puzzled me. Why *wouldn't* God heal me with modern medicine? I began to think about the stories that I had grown up loving from the Bible and the Book of Mormon: real people who had been healed in miraculous ways.

But that isn't for me, I thought immediately. *God doesn't heal people like that anymore, and if He chose to, He would heal someone far more important, or with far more influence than me. He'd heal someone that the world could see so He could showcase His work unto man.*

Something about that thought stopped me in my tracks. I wasn't talking to God anymore. I was talking to myself. Where had I heard that phrase before?

I searched "showcase His work unto man" in my phone's notes app. I often recorded spiritual thoughts and impressions there, so I figured it was the best place to start. Immediately, an entry popped up.

It was from about a month and a half earlier, when I had sat in Sunday School feeling extremely guilty for being sick and wondering if I was being punished for something I couldn't remember.

"You are not ill because you have sinned. You are ill so that God can showcase His work unto man."

Those words had been a blessing at the time, because they confirmed that I hadn't brought the illness upon myself. Those words had allowed me to let go of that anxiety and start healing emotionally.

My roommate stirred slightly, and I snapped out of my reflection.

How long had I been putting limits on my healing? How long had I been putting limits on God? I had been so convinced that God wouldn't heal me in a miraculous way because I wasn't 'important' enough. But didn't God love me just as much as He loved Lazarus or the woman with the issue of blood?

The warmth that flooded through my chest told me that He did.

And if God loved me just as much as He loved them, then who's to say that He won't heal me in just as miraculous a way?

"Heavenly Father," I began again, but stopped abruptly. It occurred to me that to anyone overhearing this prayer, I would be walking a very fine line between asking for something in faith and telling God what to do. *But God knows my heart*, I reasoned. *And I think this is what He wants too.*

The warmth in my chest grew.

"Heavenly Father," I started once again. "I'm tired. I've exhausted my options and my resources. I've been told that all that is left is for my body to recover, but it won't do that. Something's wrong and I need help. Please bless my body to begin to heal. Bless my immune system to regenerate and become strong again. Bless my joints, my organs, and my blood. Bless my nerves to repair themselves. Bless my body to be restored to it's healthy and strong state."

A thought entered my head that I wanted to reject, but it wouldn't go away. I didn't want to do anymore treatments. I wanted to be done. But the thought persisted, so I continued.

"I'll finish out my final treatments. But after that, I'm done. I'm done with doctors. I'm done with searching for answers. You're my answer. You can heal me. Please heal me." I paused briefly before adding an exasperated, "Oh, and please bless that my nose will stop bleeding so I can go to bed already. In the name of Jesus Christ, amen."

The room was very still once again. I was surprised at how normal and natural everything felt, because that prayer had been so vulnerable and candid. To be completely honest, I didn't even feel like I was the one vocalizing the words. Yes, it was my voice, but those weren't my words. I think they were His.

The entire experience couldn't have lasted more than twenty minutes, but it felt like I had been praying for hours. My eyes felt heavier than ever before, and I removed the tissue from my nose without even checking to see if the bleeding had stopped.

Somehow I knew it had.

I awoke the next morning a little disoriented. I spent a few minutes lying there, trying to remember if those early morning events had been a dream or reality.

I rolled out of bed and when my feet hit the floor, I realized something astounding: I wasn't in pain.

To anyone who hasn't experienced chronic pain, I cannot begin to describe the way *not* being in pain felt. You have to understand that at this point, it had been over nine years since I had been healthy. I hadn't been healthy since I was *ten*. I had lost the memory of what 'pain-free' felt and looked like. Prior to this moment, I literally couldn't remember a moment where nothing on my body hurt.

So when my feet hit the ground and I realized I wasn't in pain, my head cleared and I realized that the events of the previous night had not been a dream at all.

I fell to my knees and prayed, thanking God for His mercy and asking for strength to remember this experience when the pain from my treatments *did* come back.

It was a rough two months after that. Those final four treatments seemed harder on my body than all the previous treatments had ever been. I felt increasingly more exhausted. And I had days where I still felt frustrated.

But the memory of that night stayed with me, and in moments of pain I cried out to God in the name of our Savior. I reminded Him of our conversation. I asked for strength and health. And as the days turned into weeks, I could almost feel the regenerative aspects of healing begin to wake up inside me. I could quite literally feel my body begin to heal.

I finished those treatments, just as I promised, and God healed my stomach and organs, just as He promised.

And while a lot of my healing was through the blessing of modern medicine, the final and most pivotal moments came directly from God. In a way, I got my very own Bible-like miracle, and I'm still thanking God for it.

So why am I telling you this? What compelled me to share something so profound and vulnerable with perfect strangers?

There are a couple of motivating factors.

I figure that if you've made it to this point, you probably have a genuine desire to find peace or healing through Christ.

The Spirit told me I was ill to "showcase His work unto man." And I don't know if that means just me and my close friends and family, or if that includes you, sitting at the other end of this book.

My final reason for sharing this experience is that I have felt compelled to do so. And though there will probably be people who don't believe me, I know that what happened between God and me was real. I know it. He knows it. And I refuse to deny that.

God healed my illness. I'm not always pain free. I still live with fibromyalgia, so sometimes I experience aching joints or migraines. That's part of mortal life. But my decade of hardly eating to avoid pain and my ten long years of praying for a digestive system to work are over. God did that for me, and my life is drastically different because of it.

We are all broken. Whether it is physical, spiritual, or emotional, we all require healing. And with how diverse and drastic all of our individual needs are, there is only *one* physician with the capabilities to make us whole. Just one.

Jesus Christ can heal you. He can heal your body. He can heal your spirit. He can heal your heart. His grace is unlimited. His capacity to heal you is unlimited.

But are *you* limiting Him? Are you placing bounds on what He can and cannot do?

I put limitations on God that God never expressed. I decided who God was and what He was allowed to do.

I was the one who bought into the lie that God doesn't heal people out of nothing anymore. That those stories were just for the Bible and not for real life. That God could heal me that way but wouldn't because it wasn't important enough to Him.

Who am I to decide what is important to God?

Who am I to put limitations on His character and His power?

God can heal you. He wants to heal you. I can't promise that it will come now, or even in this lifetime. I have been so blessed to have this experience, but I recognize that not everyone will. Tony was taken by cancer in the prime of his life. Many friends and neighbors have been taken unexpectedly. But it doesn't make you any less faithful or any less loved. God's plan is different for all of us, and we just have to hold on to the hope that His plan is best. I can't promise that you'll be healed right now. But I can promise that as you have faith in your Savior, Jesus Christ, hope in that eventual healing will sustain you through even the darkest and lowest of times. (But if you're frustrated and angry too, that's just fine.)

This book isn't about me finally getting my ten-year miracle. It's about me having countless miracles, experiences, and blessings over the last ten years. It isn't about how I finally found the answers to my health concerns. It's about having found myself through Christ.

So I thank God for the help and healing that finally came, but I also thank God for every tear-filled, heart-wrenching moment over the last decade. I know that sounds crazy, but it's true. Exchanging my childhood and adolescent years for hospital gowns and a shattered sense of self-confidence is not how I would have chosen to spend half of my life. But that's what it was. And it caused me to plant my roots deep into the ground, weather the seemingly constant storms, and eventually bloom where I was planted.

The pain brought me to my knees in front of my Savior. The pain encouraged me to make God a priority. The pain showed me the goodness of heaven.

And however crazy it sounds, I will be forever grateful for it.

BECOMING LIKE JESUS CHRIST

TRYING TO BE LIKE JESUS

I love when my little nieces burst through the door on a Sunday afternoon, still in their church dresses, practically talking over each other to tell us what they learned. They're especially fond of teaching us the songs that they've been learning each week. It's fun to listen to them teach us songs like "Jesus Wants Me for a Sunbeam" or "A Child's Prayer."

There's something so pure about listening to children sing about Jesus. They don't even have to be good singers. (And more often than not they're off key.) But hearing them sing and proudly proclaim that they *know* Jesus loves them is beautiful and humbling in a way that makes me understand why Christ wants us to become like little children.

I remember singing those same songs, many years ago, and feeling excited to declare to our congregation that I was trying to be like Jesus.

That song in particular comes to my mind often because the older I get, the more I realize that sometimes trying to be like Jesus is really hard.

But that's our ultimate goal, isn't it? To become like Him and return home better off because of this mortal experience.

Talk about intimidating goals.

But let's be realistic for a second. When we were kids, we sang about *trying* to be like Jesus, not *being* Him. The scriptures have told us to be perfected *in* Him, not all on our own.

So why is the idea of becoming like Christ so intimidating when all we've been asked to do is *try?*

Kids are good at forgiving people and giving second chances. Kids are good at giving themselves second chances, too. When they mess up, they say sorry and genuinely try to do better. They don't waste unnecessary time feeling guilty and unworthy.

The concept of not being 'worth it' is learned.

So for this last section, I want you to try really hard to think like a little child. I want you to give yourself as much mercy and forgiveness as you would give your child or nephew or little neighbor if they hurt your feelings. I want you to show yourself the same measure of love that you would show them if they came to you with a sincere, heartfelt apology on their lips.

As we talk about becoming like Jesus Christ and making room in our hearts so that He can live in us, don't spend a single second on thoughts of failure or inadequacy. His grace is there for you whether you take it or not, so don't waste time condemning yourself for shortcomings that He died to overcome.

RECONCILIATION

A Book of Mormon prophet named Jacob admonishes us to "reconcile [ourselves] to the will of God . . . and remember . . . that it is only in and through the grace of God that [we] are saved" (2 Nephi 10:24).

We're told quite frequently that it is by grace we are saved. Grace (heavenly help, powered by love) was offered to us by the Atonement of Jesus Christ. And this grace redeems us, strengthens and comforts us, heals us, and helps us to grow and become better than we are now.

So yes, I'd agree that it is by grace that we are saved, physically, emotionally, and spiritually. Jesus Christ has truly saved us. But what I love about Jacob's commandment is that he doesn't tell us to go and qualify for grace or salvation. He doesn't tell us to earn it. He just asks us to remember it.

How often are we counselled to remember the Savior? At least once a week if we consider the sacramental prayers. But the word *remember* is used hundreds of times in the scriptures. It seems that we're almost continually being counseled to remember the goodness and grace of God.

You don't have to earn it, live up to it, or somehow buy it. You've been offered grace, so choose to accept it and remember it with gratitude.

But aside from remembering Jesus Christ in our daily lives, there are a couple of other things we can do to show our gratitude for what we have been given. Jacob talked about this too, imploring us to "reconcile [ourselves] to the will of God" (2 Nephi 10:24).

What does it mean to reconcile yourself to the will of God? I guess that depends on how you interpret the word *reconciliation*.

Some definitions of reconcile teach us that it means to harmonize or make harmonious. What would that look like in terms of a relationship with God? I imagine that it would require us to live in a way that points others to Christ. In music, harmony is not the same thing as melody, but it works to emphasize the melody in one beautiful song. We aren't perfect, and as much as we try to be like our Savior, we'll still be different and distinct. We are not Christ. We cannot offer people the same guiding melody that He can. But we can point others in His direction. We can try to use our talents and testimonies to emphasize His teachings. We can still play a vital role in His heavenly hymn.

Another definition of reconcile is to restore relations between groups of people. This is a good definition to use in reference to the repentance process. God cannot tolerate sin, so we can't return to His presence in our current state. But through the grace and Atonement of Jesus Christ, we can be made clean again. In this case, Christ is quite literally the only individual who can restore our relationship with God.

The third common interpretation of the word *reconcile* is to make something consistent with another thing. This is often used in record keeping and with bank accounts, but for our purposes, it has a lot to do with keeping our actions and thoughts consistent with the gospel of Jesus Christ. It can be used to describe our efforts to make our will align with God's will. This type of reconciliation helps you know where you stand with God, because the purpose of it is to align yourself with God as much as possible.

So how do we reconcile ourselves unto God? How do we align our will with His and live our lives in a way that allows us to point others to Christ? With such a lofty goal, how can we ever accomplish it? (Ahem, it's through grace.)

THE CHALLENGE TO BECOME

It's so hard to be like Jesus. It is often exhausting and disheartening because of how short we consistently fall. But it isn't an impossible goal. In fact, it's one of the few things I'm absolutely confident *is* possible. If we remember the grace of Jesus Christ and choose to accept Him and His Atonement, failure isn't what we should worry about. Failure isn't final with Christ, and we can always try again.

Instead, let's focus on what we do when we get back up from another failure. Let's focus on how we can change and be just a little better. Honestly, the best advice I can give is to be prayerful about it. God knows you best, and He knows what changes you and I need to make.

Recently, I felt compelled to reevaluate how I spend my time. It didn't make much sense to me at first because I was doing lots of good and necessary things. I was going to work, spending time with friends and family, and cutting back on my yearly temptation to binge watch my favorite shows all summer (or pandemic) long. But once I started really looking at how I was spending my time, I realized that I was giving God all of my leftovers. He got my leftover time. My leftover money. My leftover energy and emotions.

For pretty much the sole purpose of spiritual experimentation, I tried to change that and see what kind of difference it made. So I gave God more of me. I paid my tithing as soon as I got paid. I gave Him time throughout the day, not just in the few minutes before I fell asleep. I forced myself to kneel down to pray instead of praying while half asleep in my bed.

Honestly, it started really small. It normally takes me about twenty minutes to walk to school or work. During that time, I'd often wear headphones and listen to music to pass the time. And although that was probably just fine, I chose to switch up my routine and listen to the scriptures during my morning walks instead.

Listening to the word of the Lord early in the morning made me feel different in a way that was hard to pinpoint. I guess I just found myself more open. Throughout the day I started to find myself silently praying for help or guidance. I noticed little blessings that I had taken for granted before. Small opportunities to serve seemed to pop up everywhere, but I think that they had probably been there all along. I was just more open to them now.

Surprisingly, when I gave God the first share of time and energy, I ended up having more time and energy to finish the other important things I needed to get done, like school and work. It sounds a little counterintuitive, but it's just another example of how grace gives us power to do a little more and be a little better.

I'm not always good at giving God my time. I'm not always the best at making Him first priority. But I'm still trying because I want to be like Him one day.

I started this book with this quote from David A Bednar.

"It is one thing to know that Jesus Christ came to earth to die for us. That is fundamental and foundational to the doctrine of Christ. But we also need to appreciate that the Lord desires, through His

Atonement and by the power of the Holy Ghost, to live in us—not only to direct us but also to empower us."[1]

We often talk about how we desire to live with Him, but I think it's incredibly profound that He desires to live *in us.* He wants to reside in our hearts. He wants to play an active role in our lives. And in order for Him to do that, we have to live our lives in a way that will allow our hearts to act as temples for the Lord.

Again, that might seem a little daunting, but with His grace and guidance we *can* do it!

LOVE WHAT HE LOVES

I've always enjoyed church and have never had a problem with attendance. My parents never forced me to go. I wanted to. I knew it was right. Late into the winter of my freshman year of college, however, I decided that I did *not* want to go to church. I didn't mean permanently, of course, just on that one particularly rough morning.

I hadn't slept much the night before, and I awoke early in the morning to the blaring of an alarm I had foolishly set. No way. There was absolutely *no way* I was getting out of bed. I'd barely slept. My head was pounding. I needed the rest.

An obnoxious little voice in the back of my brain told me that I needed to get ready for church. I quite forcefully commanded that voice to shut up.

But as annoying little voices tend to keep talking, it seemed I was stuck with it.

Get out of bed. Go to church. Today is stake conference.

To be honest, I didn't care. I wasn't going. I wanted to sleep, and besides, my head *hurt.* Like really, *really* hurt.

---

1. Bednar, "In the Strength of the Lord."

Eventually I realized that my energy would be better spent pacifying my conscience, and I resolved to take a nap as soon as I got home from the meeting.

I arrived just before they began.

I found a seat next to a couple of the girls I had become friends with, nodding to them in greeting. It was still too early to talk. My head still hurt too badly to be cheerful.

I didn't pay attention to a word of the announcements, and I couldn't have repeated the name of the hymn we opened the conference with. To be honest, I didn't really tune in at all until the first speaker stood up and began his talk with, "I know that sometimes it's hard to come to church, but we do it. And the reason that we do it is because it is right."

All right, I get it, I thought.

Much to my surprise, the rest of the meeting was superb. Absolutely wonderful. I sincerely enjoyed listening to each of the speakers and found myself in a much better mood by the time it was over.

My head still hurt, but I had gone to church, learned a lot, and could now justifiably run home and take a nap.

The very next week, however, I awoke with the same annoyance and desire to skip church. This had never happened to me before. I had never actively dreaded going to church. And I didn't quite know what to do with that.

I wish I could say that I remembered the words from the week before and chose to go to church, simply because it was the right thing to do. I wish I could tell you that the speakers were once again amazing and that I felt spiritually uplifted and edified once again.

But I can't. Because guess what? I turned off my alarm, rolled over, and went back to sleep. Or rather, I *tried* to go back to sleep.

The words were in my head before I had even had the chance to drift back into unconsciousness.

"Are we going to have this argument every week?"

Anyone who says that God doesn't have a sense of humor is lying. Or at least they do not know the same God I know. In all honesty, though, I don't think God was *trying* to be funny. I think He was probably genuinely annoyed at my lack of effort (and lack of learning from the previous week).

But despite the fact that He was probably reasonably disappointed in me, I started to laugh because truly, I had not expected that response.

So you know what? I went to church. And the speakers were all perfectly ordinary and mundane. I remember nothing else particularly noteworthy from that day. But I had gone, and this time I had learned my lesson.

Sometimes we don't have it in us to *want* to go to church. Sometimes we just don't have the desire to read our scriptures or to pray. Sometimes we just want to be left alone.

On those days, I try to remind myself that it's okay to feel that way. Yes, we should love what the Lord loves, but when we can't do that, we should just strive to do as He does.

Sometimes that's still going to be difficult, but it is more doable.

If your desire to come unto Christ has gone out, know that I've been there. I know that it will come back. It might take weeks, months, or even years, but it *will* come back. The love you once felt for Him and His gospel will return, but not without effort.

So keep trying. Keep believing. Keep doing what is right, simply because it is right. As you do what the Lord does, you *will* come to love what He loves too.

GROUNDING YOURSELF

Over the years, I've been asked a lot of "sick girl questions." At least, that's what I like to call them. These are the kinds of questions that people wouldn't bring up in a typical conversation with their healthy friends. It would be weird. But when you're consistently sick, people talk to you differently.

I was never greeted with an ordinary, "How are you?" Instead, I was met with one of these.

What are your symptoms today?

How is your health?

Have you eaten recently?

When was the last time you went to the doctor?

Or my personal favorite:

Have they figured out what's wrong with you yet?

Naturally, all of these questions were asked out of love and with a genuine concern for my well-being, so I ignored the potentially offensive connotations of their words and answered politely.

It was weird at first, talking so openly about all the ways in which my body was failing me. It was odd to receive messages from strangers who had heard about my issues from a mutual friend, and it was even more surprising when those messages supplied information from similar cases and potential treatments to look into. It was humbling, although surprising, to see that so many people cared, but it felt wrong to have a plethora of people invade my privacy.

But some health issues are hard to hide, so I gave up trying and eventually started a blog to keep everyone updated at once. It didn't stop the questions, though.

But not all the questions were awkward or embarrassing. In fact, some of them were quite humbling.

As I began to post public updates on social media, I tried really hard to honestly depict my situation. I didn't hide the pain or heartache. Not at all. But I also wanted to highlight the tender mercies I was seeing day to day, because it helped to ground me.

And much to my surprise, my efforts to post real, cautiously optimistic updates on my health issues impacted people. But it wasn't until much later that I started getting asked the kind questions that humbled me.

How do you manage to stay so hopeful despite your pain?

How do you keep yourself steady in the gospel?

What advice do you have for other people who want to get to know Jesus Christ for themselves?

These questions startled me because I didn't think my relationship with Jesus Christ was different from anyone else's. It wasn't until much later that I realized just how unique my adolescent years had been and how they had pushed me to seek our Savior more actively than I otherwise would have had I been healthy.

Still, I don't feel particularly qualified to answer those questions.

Your relationship with heaven is unique to you. I couldn't possibly direct or make judgments about it. I wouldn't even know where to begin.

What I *can* do is tell you the things that have helped me. I can give you a list of ideas on how to study differently, or direct you to resources that you can turn to for guidance. My suggestions might not be the right fit for you, but sometimes it's helpful to brainstorm ideas, particularly if you don't know where to begin.

FINDING YOUR FAITH: LINE UPON LINE

Gratitude Prayers

I know a lot of people keep gratitude journals, but honestly, I've never been good at that. Instead, I sometimes choose to say gratitude prayers. I pray to Heavenly Father and do nothing except thank Him for the blessings in my life. This is a good one to do on a day you're feeling particularly blessed, as well as on the days when you're struggling to see God in your life at all.

It starts off a little difficult, particularly if you've had a bad day. I remember the nights when I could only tell God I was grateful for my family, my house, and just the general existence of dogs. I couldn't think of anything else to be grateful for. (On those particularly rough days, I sometimes extend my goal and choose to only say gratitude prayers for a week straight. It puts things in perspective really fast, and you'll be amazed at how many blessings you already have.)

God's Notes versus My Notes

This is a brilliant idea that was supplied to me by one of my old teachers. It's a note-taking strategy that has changed how I listen to devotionals or study my scriptures. And all you need is a blank sheet of paper and a pen.

Divide the sheet of paper into two columns, labelling the first one *My Notes* and the second one *God's Notes.*

In the first column, write down the things you think are interesting or important (specific quotes, main ideas, scriptures referenced, and so on). In the other column, write down spiritual impressions that come into your head. (If you aren't sure if it's an impression, follow Tony's advice and write it down anyway!) Most of the notes I put in this column have to do with people I should reach out to, topics I should study in more detail, or changes I need to make to my life. Sometimes they have nothing to do with the actual text I'm studying.

Studying like this has provided a night and day difference in my spiritual growth, and I am indebted to whoever came up with this method. You rock!

Short-Term Goals Lead to Success

My problem sticking to goals is less of a persistence problem and more of an *I'm being unreasonable* problem. For example, I once decided that there was no excuse for me missing my daily scripture study and that I wouldn't miss a day from then on for the rest of my life.

What? Liv, no.

Not surprisingly, I failed at that goal.

But then I rephrased it. I told myself that for the next three days I would study my scriptures, and suddenly that was more doable. After three days I upped it to one week and then two. Eventually I went a month without missing my scripture study, and then two and three. It was much easier to make the changes I wanted to make when I kept my goals small and attainable, and then *slowly* built my way up.

That being said, remember grace. You will occasionally mess up and that's okay. Forgive yourself and try again.

Record Keeping Is a Game Changer

I said that I'm terrible at keeping a gratitude journal, but that was a lie. In reality, I'm terrible at keeping *any* kind of journal. I've tried so many times, and I haven't yet found a way to make it stick. (Even when I've tried to set small goals. I'm just really, really bad at journal keeping. If you have suggestions, please send them my way!)

But keeping a record is important, isn't it? If I hadn't kept some sort of record, I never would have remembered that time when God reassured me that I wasn't sick to be punished for something. And that was an important thing for me to remember.

So the best way I've found to keep a record without actually keeping a journal is by keeping a notes app on my phone. Every time I receive revelation, chastisement, or a prompting to do something that I cannot do right away, I enter it into the app. It doesn't make up for a journal, and my grandkids and I will never know what I did after school on September 13, 2016, but at least I'll have a record of things that impacted me spiritually in case I ever need to fall back on them.

Stay Quiet . . . Seriously

Although my family claims that I'm frequently jabbering on, I still don't understand why people feel the need to fill *every* silence with noise. Silence isn't bad. It shouldn't be uncomfortable or unwelcome. In fact, I think a little bit of silence can be good for us. It gives us time to think, and it gives the Spirit uninterrupted space to speak to us. We just need to listen.

I'm not saying we should take up a vow of silence and refuse to speak to one another. I'm just saying that allotting ten to fifteen minutes a day for quiet meditation might help you decompress and feel a little more in tune with your spirit and *the* Spirit.

Creativity Is an Attribute of Heaven

My last suggestion is to be creative. I'm a huge believer that creative acts can connect you with heaven. That's part of the reason I started writing. I just needed a creative outlet. I've tried to take up other creative arts as well, no matter how poorly I advanced. My sketching and painting skills are pretty much non-existent, but eventually I learned that writing (or even just playing) music could offer me the spiritual reset I needed every once in a while.

For those of you saying that you aren't creative, I'm prepared to argue with you. God is creative. He created you and me and the planet that we call home. Creativity is in our DNA as children of God.

Maybe art isn't your thing but baking is. Or perhaps you enjoy gardening or building structures from Legos. Puzzle games or photography or restoring cars could also be considered creative acts. In fact, I can think of several ways in which math and science could also be considered creative releases.

The point is that there are a million things you and I could do to be creative, and I think it's important to do something. You don't have to do it every day either. But sometimes our minds need a break from day-to-day life, and we need a little recreational time. (Plus participating in creative hobbies gives you a good opportunity to take that quiet time I mentioned earlier.)

Israel, Israel, God Is Calling

I've always loved the imagery of our Savior calling out to His lambs, or the depiction of Him knocking on our door, hoping we'll answer and let Him inside. I love the idea that He isn't just waiting for us but is actively calling for us, searching for us, and inviting us home.

The scriptures are full of stories where God calls out to His people, commanding them to move across the world or build up temples across the lands. He directed His people and called out to them then, and He directs and cries out to us now.

Can you hear Him? What is He saying to you?

I've spent many years experimenting with my spirituality, testing gospel principles, and building a foundation of experiences that I could fall back on if doubts ever came. I have laughed, cried, and been stunned into silence because of the glory and majesty of God and His plan for us. I've worked hard to establish and maintain a personal relationship with my Savior and my Heavenly Father. I've spent *years* learning what the whisperings of the Spirit feel like to me personally. It has been the longest, hardest, and most worthwhile journey of my life, and I'm nowhere near done.

But despite the fact that I still have so much work to do, I cannot help but thank God for the progress He has helped me make and for the experiences that He has allowed me to have.

It couldn't have been easy for God, as my Father, to allow me to suffer pain and heartbreak. It couldn't have felt good to Him when I was angry and placing the blame on His back. It must have been difficult to see me so lost and confused, and it probably still is, because I'm still quite often unsure of where I'm going. When God gave us His Son, He gave us His heart. And although my heart was breaking from the pain I was experiencing over a decade, His heart was broken from day one.

We talk about our hearts a lot. We say that we need to hand them over to God. And I believe that. But with the creation of the plan of happiness, God gave us *His* heart. He gave us the power to *hurt* Him. He opened Himself up to pain. He watched His Son suffer and cry out to Him in anguish. He watched Him die. He constantly watches His children blame Him, hate Him, and turn away from Him. He allows us to abuse the agency we have. He permits us to belittle and deny Him.

I can't believe He loves us enough to let us hurt Him like that.

I once had a peculiar dream that I still find myself thinking about quite often. It was simple, as far as dreams go. I was standing outside of a church building, under the shade of a tree with my friends. We were waiting for a meeting or an activity to start.

My friends and I were talking about the gospel and about how much the Lord must love His people if He was willing to die for them.

Jeffrey R. Holland appeared behind us, as people tend to do in dreams. "You have no idea," he inserted quietly.

We turned to him questioningly.

"You have no idea how much the Lord knows and loves you, or how much we, as a quorum, know and love you."

He turned and walked inside the building, and I awoke with the feeling that he had been speaking right to me.

I believe that. I believe that the Lord knows and loves you. I believe that our leaders know and love us. I believe that our future is bright and that you and I are going to be okay.

I testify that God lives and loves you more than you can understand or believe. He sent His Son to atone for you, to *die* for you, so that you could live again and so you never have to go without comfort, strength, or company. Jesus Christ is your Savior, our Savior, and He knows you intimately. This is His gospel, and it is as perfect as He is.

I bear witness that He extends His grace to all who have even the smallest degree of faith, or the tiniest desire to change. His grace is for you. His Atonement is for you. His gospel is for you. There is a place for you here. There is an important work for you specifically to do.

You have talents. You have gifts that enable you to be the Lord's hands and do His work here on earth. So stand up. Stand out from the world. Be different in the most positive of ways and reconcile yourself with the Lord so that He may live in you.

This is my hope for you, and for me, and for my future family that might come across this one day. You are the Lord's legacy. You are His finest soldiers. Your impact is real and your participation is necessary.

So let's march out together, stand our ground, and take comfort in knowing that *every* moment we spend keeping our covenants, serving a neighbor, or reading our scriptures, He is not only here on Earth with us but living in us.

LOVING OUR GOD

The first commandment is to love God with everything in us; with everything we have. Christ taught us about that in the New Testament, but He's been telling His people to love God since the beginning of mankind.

But the thing is, I didn't always love God. I actively hated Him. And after spending time in the scriptures, trying to act as Christ would and eventually coming to love God, I felt guilty for that.

I had blamed Him for everything in those early days. Every test that led nowhere. Every doctor who gave up on me and said they were out of ideas. I blamed Him for that. I blamed Him for the anguish that I felt in both my body and my soul because I'd never experienced anything like it before.

I blamed Him for not letting me get better. I blamed Him for letting me remain in darkness, in pain, and in misery. I blamed him for taking away my childhood.

When I finally grew to love Him (and by the way, that love grew by inches and not miles in the beginning), I started to hate myself for being so rash and angry.

Once I understood the nature of God, I learned that He didn't cause my pain, and though He didn't stop it, He still loved me. Mortality is a brutal thing. There's heartbreak and soul-crushing disappointment everywhere you turn. If you aren't experiencing it, I guarantee your neighbor is.

But there's love in there too. God sent me little love notes over and over again to remind me that He cared. Occasionally, He gave me the gift of sleeping through the night, a rarity with my medical conditions. Sometimes He'd send friends or neighbors to check in on me and to help me know that as much as I felt alone, I wasn't really.

It always made me wonder if Christ had friends and neighbors who checked up on Him when He was at His lowest. But unfortunately, I don't think He got the same tender mercies that we did. He had to atone for us entirely alone.

I'm still learning to forgive myself for putting so much effort into hating God, although I'm fully aware that He is not angry at me. Still, the best idea I can come up with for helping me forgive myself is by loving Him as hard as I can now and each day moving forward.

So how can I love God? What would help Him see how much gratitude I feel for Him? Aside from my words, what else is there?

LOVING OUR NEIGHBOR

I think that one of the best ways we can show God our love is by loving others. After all, they're His children too. He created them. He loves them. And if we want to be like Him, we need to love what (and who) He loves.

Unfortunately, we're all rather terrible at loving each other. Sure, we love our neighbors or our friends. That's convenient love. But what about inconvenient love?

I see the most divisive actions in political and religious spheres. Across political beliefs and religious denominations, we forget to love our neighbor because our neighbor doesn't think the same way we do.

I think the Lord would be disappointed in us for that.

Do you remember the story of the good Samaritan? It's a story of a man forgotten by his own people but loved and cared for by his perceived enemy. Growing up, I always loved this story because it showcases what love should look like. Love does not depend on sharing beliefs. Love does not depend on living the same lifestyle.

But it isn't just the good Samaritan that teaches us to love one another. The Lord Himself spent most of His time with the sinners and outcasts because He knew they deserved love too.

The Bible frequently commands us to love our neighbors *and* our enemies.

I don't think God can get much clearer on what He wants from us: love one another, full stop. Love without conditions. Leave the condemnation to God.

LETTING GOD LOVE US

Aside from loving the people and things that God has created, I think one of the best ways that we can show love to God is by letting Him love us, and by loving ourselves in return.

How often do we proclaim that we are our own worst enemies? How often do we look in the mirror, scroll through social media, and decide that we aren't as pretty, faithful, or talented as somebody else?

We hate ourselves, and that is offensive to God.

God made us. He made us the way He wanted us and gave us the attributes that would allow us to serve a unique role on the earth. And He doesn't make mistakes.

We can honor God by honoring ourselves as children of God. We can take care of our bodies and our minds. We can feed our spirits. We can praise God for the beauty that He put in us.

Loving yourself is hard. I struggle with it daily. But I don't want to offend God by mocking or belittling what He created when He made me. So I pray often for help to love myself better and to know how to take care of my body, mind, and soul.

God will answer those prayers. He wants you to love yourself. He wants you to see yourself the way He sees you.

CHEERFUL CHRISTIANITY

BECOMING A CHEERFUL CHRISTIAN

We came to this earth to become like our Heavenly Parents in every way possible. First, we needed to receive a body of flesh and blood, just like theirs. We needed to form families and make connections because that is at the center of His plan for us. But we also needed to obtain knowledge, use our agency to choose Him, and do our best to become something more than we were at the start of this journey. But none of those things can happen without pain, heartbreak, and sorrow.

Misery is an essential ingredient for happiness.

When Adam and Eve were cast out of the garden, the Lord talked about how they would eat sorrow for the rest of their days and that the earth would be cursed for their sakes. This might sound like an incredibly harsh punishment from a vengeful and unloving God, but I don't see it that way anymore. The Lord says He would do these things *for their sake*. Those things are for them. Their benefit. Their growth.

God loved them so much that He not only provided a Savior to save them from their mistakes, but He also took a painful situation and turned it into a learning experience.

And it *was* a painful situation, for both them and God.

Adam and Eve were cast out of the garden, but God had to cast them out, knowing that by doing so, some of his children would not choose to come back home to Him.

I cannot imagine anything *more* painful. And yet, even in His pain, He was merciful to us. He provided us with every opportunity to be better, giving us a Savior for when we fall short, and allowing us a lifetime of opportunities to use our own judgment and agency, with grace available when we use that judgement and agency poorly.

The gospel is so unfair in our favor. I don't think I'll ever stop being amazed at it.

So, despite the fact that I'm healthy for the first time since elementary school, I am not done. My learning and growth will continue on for the rest of my life. I'm grateful for that because if I stopped progressing right where I'm at now, I'd never become like my Heavenly Parents.

If you see me on the street and ask me how I'm doing, I might say great. Or I might tear up and tell you that I'm tired and frustrated. I might be angry at my circumstances. I might refuse to be optimistic and let myself wallow for a few days. Heck, I've given people all of those answers in the last few weeks alone. But ultimately, I'll raise my chin up and continue onward, because onward is upward, and upward is home.

And that's what this is really about. Every trial of faith. Every lesson in grace. Every tear. Every smile. Every blessing. Every curse on the ground that's for our sake. It's all about home and getting back there better (not perfect), but better than we were before. Being a cheerful Christian is about the journey home. It's about learning from difficult circumstances, feeling the full range of human emotions, and developing a relationship with our Savior.

Cheerful Christianity does not require a constantly cheerful disposition. It requires faith in our Savior and hope that He can make us whole again, no matter the things we've done.

I am a cheerful Christian. I hope you'll become one too.

ACKNOWLEDGMENTS

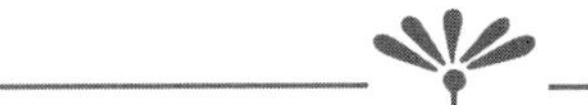

I never understood the purpose of an acknowledgments section until I began writing this book. In that process I learned that it truly does take a village. I'll forever be grateful to my parents for raising me to be a cheerful Christian, and to the rest of my family for their patience and support through all of my sick years, random ambitions, and daunting projects.

I'm grateful for Tony and for his beautiful wife, Erica, who gave me permission to share a bit about him and his insights that have helped shape what I believe about God.

To my friends, who have stood by me through all my writer's block and moments of imposter syndrome, and who have never stopped believing in this book, even when I had.

To Kelsea Smellie for the beautiful photography. Thank you.

To TJ Moore, for helping me understand the life and ministry of Christ from a more personal perspective, and for helping me to consider my life decisions from a greater, eternal perspective.

I'd like to offer a special thanks to Hank Smith and Anthony Sweat, who mentored me through the publishing process and encouraged me to never give up or forget the importance of this project. They have helped me find the confidence to share my story with you.

I'd be remiss if I failed to thank my Savior, Jesus Christ, for dying so that I could live, and for understanding me when no when else can. Without Him, neither I nor this book would be sitting in front of you.

And to my Heavenly Parents, whom I adore and miss, I want to offer the greatest praise and gratitude. Without Their patience and persistent insistence, I would have never written this, nor would I have grown in the ways that writing this book has allowed me to. I am only myself because of Them, and Their confidence in me is one of the greatest blessings I have experienced.

To my readers: thank you. Thank you for your support. Thank you for letting me tell my story, and for respecting the Spirit that guided me through this process. Without you, I am just a young woman, writing to the void.

You are my everything.

ABOUT THE AUTHOR

Olivia Ruth Barney was born into the house of two God-loving parents and a small army of siblings. She spends her time sharing thoughtful and inspiring messages for Christian adults and youth around the world. She spent eleven painful years seeking the solace of a savior, all while battling unexpected health issues, the loss of family members, and bullying by the hands of friends and teachers. She runs a website and social media platforms dedicated to silver linings and the endless pursuit of Jesus.

LET'S CONNECT

For continued content, updates on new releases, or the simple opportunity to chat, connect with me online.

Instagram: @oliviaruthbarney
Facebook: /oliviaruthbarney

More study resources, blog posts, and thoughts about Christianity can be found at **www.oliviaruthbarney.com**.

Scan to visit

www.oliviaruthbarney.com